# MIDNIGHT IN SAMARRA

## THE TRUE STORY OF WMD, GREED, AND HIGH CRIMES IN IRAQ

### FRANK GREGORY FORD WITH ELEANOR COONEY

HOT BOOKS

Hot Books may be purchased in bulk at special discounts for sales promotion, corporate gifts, fund-raising, or educational purposes. Special editions can also be created to specifications. For details, contact the Special Sales Department, Skyhorse Publishing, 307 West 36th Street, 11th Floor, New York, NY 10018 or info@skyhorsepublishing.com.

Hot Books® and Skyhorse Publishing® are registered trademarks of Skyhorse Publishing, Inc., a Delaware corporation.

Visit our website at www.hotbookspress.com.

10 9 8 7 6 5 4 3 2 1

Library of Congress Cataloging-in-Publication Data is available on file.

Cover design by Paul Qualcom

Print ISBN: 978-1-5107-4020-4
Ebook ISBN: 978-1-5107-4021-1

Printed in the United States of America

# CONTENTS

# CONTENTS

# FOREWORD

## By David Talbot

The world is burning, and yet the firelight illuminates the way out. The times are dire, even catastrophic. Nonetheless we can sense a grand awakening, a growing realization all around the globe that "people have the power, to dream, to rule, to wrestle the world from fools" in the prophetic words of Patti Smith.

But in order to rouse ourselves from the nightmares that hold us in their grip, we need to know more about the forces that bedevil us, the structures of power that profit from humanity's exploitation and from that of the earth. That's the impetus behind Hot Books, a series that seeks to expose the dark operations of power and to light the way forward.

Skyhorse publisher Tony Lyons and I started Hot Books in 2015 because we believe that books can make a difference. Since then the Hot Books series has shined a light on the cruel reign of racism and police violence in Baltimore (D. Watkins' *The Beast Side*); the urgent need to hold US officials accountable for their criminal actions during the war on terror (Rachel Gordon's *American Nuremberg*); the poisoning of US soldiers by their own environmentally reckless commanding officers (Joseph Hickman's *The Burn Pits*); the covert manipulation of the media by intelligence agencies (Nicholas Schou's *Spooked*); the rise of a rape culture on campus (Kirby Dick and Amy Ziering's *The Hunting Ground*); the insidious demonizing of Muslims in the media and in Washington (Arsalan Iftikhar's *Scapegoats*); the crackdown on whistleblowers who know the government's dirty secrets (Mark Hertsgaard's *Bravehearts*); the disastrous policies of the liberal elite that led to the triumph of Trump (Chris Hedges' *Unspeakable*); the American wastelands that gave rise to this dark reign (Alexander Zaitchik's *The Gilded Rage*); the energy titans and their political servants who are threatening human survival (Dick Russell's *Horsemen of the Apocalypse*); the utilization of authoritarian tactics by Donald Trump that threaten to erode American democracy (Brian Klaas's *The Despot's Apprentice*); the capture, torture, and detention of the first "high-value target" captured by the CIA after 9/11 (Joseph Hickman and John Kiriakou's *The Convenient Terrorist*); the deportation of American veterans (J. Malcolm Garcia's *Without a Country*); the ways in which our elections have failed, and continue to fail, their billing as model democracy (Steven Rosenfeld's *Democracy Betrayed*); the unexplored failures of government officials to use available intelligence to stop the events of September 11th (John Duffy and Ray Nowosielski's *The Watchdogs Didn't Bark*); the "dirty tricks" that undermined democracy during the Nixon years and destroyed public trust in politics during the seventies (Shane O'Sullivan's *Dirty Tricks*); and the war crimes and atrocities committed against not one, but countless soldiers (Frank Gregory Ford and Eleanor Cooney's *Midnight in Samarra*). And the series continues, going where few publishers dare.

Hot Books are more condensed than standard-length books. They're packed with provocative information and points of view that mainstream publishers usually shy from. Hot Books are meant not just to stir readers' thinking, but to stir trouble.

Hot Books authors follow the blazing path of such legendary muckrakers and troublemakers as Upton Sinclair, Lincoln Steffens, Rachel Carson, Jane Jacobs, Jessica Mitford, I.F. Stone and Seymour Hersh. The magazines and newspapers that once provided a forum for this deep and dangerous journalism have shrunk in number and available resources. Hot Books aims to fill this crucial gap.

American journalism has become increasingly digitized and commodified. If the news isn't fake, it's usually shallow. But there's a growing hunger for information that is both credible and undiluted by corporate filters.

A publishing series with this intensity cannot keep burning in a vacuum. Hot Books needs a culture of equally passionate readers. Please spread the word about these titles—encourage your bookstores to carry them, post comments about them in online stores and forums, persuade your book clubs, schools, political groups and community organizations to read them and invite the authors to speak.

It's time to go beyond this packaged news and propaganda. It's time for Hot Books . . . journalism without borders.

"I know where Saddam Hussein is hiding," said the Sheik, so calmly and casually as he made himself comfortable on my camel-hide sofa that it could only have been the truth. "I can tell you where he is and how to capture him."

He'd appeared unannounced, as usual. I'd known by the studied, deliberate way he extracted a Gauloises from its gold case, examined it, tapped it, lit it, inhaled and exhaled while he chose his words that whatever he was going to tell me was big.

And indeed, this was a bit of information I didn't think even the Balad bureaucrats would be able to slough off.

Trying to stay casual myself, I came to hyper-alert attention. Not only was this distinguished man the titular Sheik of the Saladin Province, which included the territory from Samarra to Tikrit and all the surrounding Tigris River area, he had known Saddam since they were children. Everything he'd told me so far had proven to be true and of incalculable value. I'd heard rumors that the CIA wanted to get their hands on the Sheik. If that were to happen, I knew all too bitterly well what his fate might be.

"Why would you reveal Saddam's whereabouts?" I asked, because I was genuinely curious. "Doing so puts your life in grave danger."

"My life and the lives of my people are in danger anyway," he answered. "The trouble and complication caused by Saddam's presence in our midst adds exponentially to that danger. I want him out of there." He paused, then added: "Besides, his day is done."

# MIDNIGHT IN
# SAMARRA

# CHAPTER 1

# WILD BLUE

June 26, 2003: the Wright brothers could never in their most delirious dreams have imagined the roaring, hulking leviathan—descendant of their first flimsy little wood-and-cloth flying machine, mighty engines turning, ready to take to the sky—that sat on the runway in Balad, Iraq that day. And anyone who's never seen a military Medevac plane can hardly imagine it, either. It's literally a flying intensive care hospital, bigger than a 747, bristling with the most advanced medical equipment in the world and designed to airlift a couple of hundred wounded warriors at a time out of the battle zone.

You'd think a species that could invent all of that—the plane, the mind-boggling trauma medicine, the computers, technology, training and communications supporting it all—could invent a way to stop war in the first place so there'd be no need for any of this. Problem is, we'd have to *want* to stop war. I'm sorry to have to report the bad news: our overlords, those Masters of War Bob Dylan sang about a few decades ago, have no wish to stop it. Why would they want to stop something so profitable and exciting? *Stop* it? Hell, no. They love it.

This was a truth I'd learned hard and well in my three months in Iraq, about to come to an abrupt end as I stood on the broiling tarmac, under guard, my weapons forcibly and illegally taken away from me, waiting to board the Medevac flight. The Delta Force commando assigned to me to make sure I didn't make a break for it or lunge for someone's throat or maybe try to grab a weapon or pull some other B-movie-type stunt muttered just loud enough for me to hear him over the whine of the engines:

"This is pure bullshit."

"You got that right," I muttered back.

The sight of me standing there, intact and uninjured, on my own two legs under my own power, duffel bags in hand, brought an irate Airman down the rear ramp. The plane was loaded, ready to take off, but had been delayed so it could take on one more "patient": me.

"What's this?" the Airman demanded. "This guy looks perfectly healthy. He's walking, carrying his own bags. What the hell's going on here?"

Captain Pia Navarro, MD (not her real name), who'd been watching for my arrival like a bride at the altar who thinks maybe the groom might bail, stepped forward and put her ninety-seven-pound self between me and the Airman.

"I can't tell you," she said, trying to put as much authority into her voice as she could muster. By now, I knew exactly what her "authority" was worth. "It's classified," she added importantly. "I can't talk about it."

"This is a Medevac flight. It's for sick and wounded *only*." The Airman glared, looking me up and down. "This guy's not getting on this plane!" Navarro winced at the force of his words. She'd already done a lot of wincing that day.

"I have to talk to the pilot." She hurried up the ramp and disappeared into the plane while we all stood there—me, the commando, the Airman, the driver who'd brought me there—at a stalemate. I said nothing, though I tried to convey to the Airman with my expression that none of this was my idea.

I don't know what she said to the pilot, but it didn't take more than a couple of minutes for a Jeep to come speeding along the runway to where we were standing, four fully locked-and-loaded MPs (military police) leaping out before the driver had even screeched to a full stop.

They surrounded me. One of the MPs carried a stretcher and plunked it down on the runway.

"Get on it!" he barked.

"No fucking way," I said, my blood rising. I was feeling less and less like obeying orders from anybody, much less this high school dropout.

"Please," Navarro flat out pleaded now, her eyes oozing tears. "Please, please, just lie down on the stretcher. That's all you have to do. You can't get on the plane if you're not on the stretcher. I'm begging you. Please don't make me force you."

"*Force* me?" I gave a bitter laugh. "I guess you know something about force, huh?" Then I leaned in. Not too much, not enough to make the MPs jump me, but enough to let her know I meant business. I saw her flinch, draw back, and I almost felt sorry for her. Almost. The MPs stiffened, eager as trained Dobermans, just barely restraining themselves. "You," I said, pointing a finger but not touching her. "You've been cowed. Duped. You let Segura totally bulldoze you. And the worst part of it is that you *know* it."

"Please," she begged again. "I'll explain it all to you later. Just lie down on the stretcher. Just for a couple of minutes. That's all."

"You realize," I said, drilling a look right into her eyes, "that you, a psychiatrist, an MD, have rank over anybody, even a General, when it comes to any medical decision. In fact, you're *required* to overrule anyone who oversteps. You're letting a Captain, a non-MD, a non-shrink, a guy barely qualified to change a tire, make a diagnosis that you *know* is hogwash and then bully you into going with it! You could be court-martialed for any part of this. For letting him shout you down, for caving in, for lying on medical forms. Can you spell malpractice? Where do your crimes start? Where do they finish?"

I guess I convinced her I wasn't just making idle chitchat, because next thing I knew she gave a small but definite sign to the MPs, who rushed forward and grabbed me. When they did, something inside of me kind of deflated. *What the hell,* I thought; *it's not like I want to stay in this garden spot even another ten seconds.*

"Okay, guys," I said, lifting my hands like the Pope in mid-benediction. "Okay, okay, okay." Disappointed, they relaxed their grip. I got onto the stretcher and lay there as they strapped me down and jerked the buckles into place with a little more force than necessary. Who could blame them? I'd deprived them of the fun of knocking my legs out from under me and doing a Rodney King beatdown right there on the runway, maybe even putting a bullet or two in me. Then I was lifted, carried up the ramp and into the plane, Navarro hurrying along next to us.

I felt pretty foolish, being carried perfectly able-bodied on a stretcher into the company of actual wounded soldiers, some in grave condition, others less so, but all of them hurt, who themselves lay on stretchers in tiers, a sort of bunk-bed arrangement along the two sides of the plane's huge interior. There were IV lines and oxygen tanks, banks of blinking and flashing monitoring devices, and busy attentive medical personnel, everyone crisp and organized and professional under the fluorescent lights. That was the Air Force for you—always several cuts above. Certainly light-years above the band of criminals, clowns, and incompetents whose company I'd been keeping these last few months.

I was put in one of the tiers. The MPs exited, the rear hatch was closed, orders were relayed, personnel got into place. The engines revved and the plane started its pre-takeoff maneuvers. We'd barely begun taxiing when Navarro came and stood over me, both hands gripping the bunk rail above. She heaved a big sigh, no doubt meant to make me feel pity for her plight and make me think she was worried about me at the same time. I just looked back at her stonily. I was a trained intelligence agent; I knew how to read the minute involuntary twitches of facial muscles and fleeting shadows of expressions, all beyond our conscious control. What I saw on her face behind the mask of concern was a mix of guilt, terror, and vexed self-pity. And I thought, but didn't say: *You got yourself into this, baby. If you think I'm going to help you get out of it, think again.*

She undid the straps. The mere fact that she did this was further proof that she knew perfectly well I wasn't crazy. What psychiatrist would let a delusional loon loose on a Medevac flight? I could run amok, attack her, tear out IV lines. I wouldn't, though, and she knew it.

"Come sit with me," she said, looking around to make sure no one could hear. "I have something to tell you. Something I'll deny if I'm ever asked about it."

Well, this was certainly intriguing. We went and sat out of earshot of others. Not that anyone was trying to eavesdrop; they were too busy tending to their vital duties, though I detected interested glances in our direction as I rose from my stretcher.

Navarro sighed again. She was good at those big sighs. Probably used them all her life, I thought. But I was ready to hear whatever it was she was about to say.

"This had better be good," I said with measured calm, buckling my seatbelt for takeoff.

"It was Col. Maloney who arranged all of this." *Gosh, what a surprise,* I almost said. "He had to get you out of the country as fast as he could, by any means he could." She paused. I waited. "He's scared to death of everything you're saying."

# CHAPTER 2

# THE DOGS OF WAR

## CAMP VIRGINIA, KUWAIT, MARCH 14, 2003

*Nothing reveals the size and scope of the war machine like the night.* These were my thoughts as I gazed into the vast darkness from high atop a guard tower near the Iraq border. I watched the steady river of lights of thousands of supply trucks moving north bumper-to-bumper along the highway, starting at the Port of Kuwait and stretching thirty-five or forty miles beyond the border into Iraq. I saw the lights of plane after plane taking off from Kuwait, also heading north, and the occasional eerie flare of cruise missiles fired over Iraq. The distances were so great, and the night so clear, that this infinite 3-D light show took place in surreal silence. If I didn't know what I was looking at, the panorama of flaring, arcing, winking, shimmering, flowing lights on the ground, in the air and in the sky as far as I could see, the almost-full moon presiding over it all, would have seemed beautiful, almost festive. The "official" beginning of the war would not happen for another week or so, but the invasion was already well underway, had been for months, a gargantuan game board carefully laid out, long before George W. Bush ceremonially whipped the starter flag down.

Have you ever seen the pyramids at Giza by moonlight? I have, from the window of the C5-A military transport plane that brought us to Kuwait just a couple of days earlier. The cool light of the waxing moon cast the pyramids' ancient geometry in sharp relief. In their thousands of years of existence, how many other armies had they seen come and go? How many more would they see long after we were gone? As we flew steadily eastward, I was aware of entering a part of the world with more than its share of the old Seven Wonders. We were headed directly into the heart of what's called the cradle of civilization: Mesopotamia, where math, astronomy, medicine, engineering, agriculture, art, and law had been thriving while Europeans were running around in skins and reading animal entrails. The sight of the pyramids in the moonlight would become a permanent image in the gallery of my memory.

Some memories, like the pyramids, I'll be telling my grandchildren about. Others not so much. Here's a different image I'll always be stuck with, almost as vivid: the trash and chaos left behind in the C5-A after the eighteen-hour flight landed and emptied out. An astonished Airman asked me who was responsible for cleaning up the mess; I, in the interest of good public relations, volunteered. It took me a couple of hours and I filled four big trash bags with cans, bottles, pizza crusts, chicken bones, food and candy wrappers, milk cartons, and mustard and ketchup packets, all heedlessly scattered on the floor—everywhere, including up in the officers' section. I mopped up spilt Coke and milk. I was pretty disgusted. Where was the order, judgment, and sense of duty the military was supposedly famous for? The squared-away discipline, the *esprit de corps* that should set soldiers apart from the regular citizens they used to be? This was like a frat house after a keg party. *Not an auspicious start for our exalted mission*, I thought while I bent over to sweep litter out from under the seats. That had not been my first inkling of unease.

On this night, I'd been ordered up into the guard tower by my commanding officer, Lt. Col. Craig Maloney (not his real name). He seemed to get a particular kick out of assigning me—a noncommissioned officer, intelligence agent, medic, and combat engineer, older than he was by almost ten years—to lowly or menial tasks, just because he could. KP duty ("kitchen police" or "kitchen patrol") was one of his favorites. He'd also ordered me to burn barrels of sewage. The lowlier the task, the happier he was. And he didn't mind putting a valuable agent in unnecessary danger. A lot of money had been invested in my training; putting me up in the guard tower, where I could have been picked off by a sniper, would have wiped out that investment in a split second. He liked, way too much, the power of being able to bark a few words and be obeyed. Did I feel singled out? Not necessarily. Picture this: zero hour on the tarmac at Ft. Bragg,

NC. Several hundred troops, fully loaded with gear and weapons, lined up, ready to board the C5-A that'll carry us to the other side of the world, some of us quite possibly to our deaths.

Along comes Col. Maloney, looking pissy. And he gives an order: a search through the officers' duffel bags to find his own, while everyone stands at attention. The bags have already been loaded; now they are unloaded, one by one, until his bag is found. When it is, he rifles through it like a peeved toddler, right there in front of all of us.

And what, you might ask, was so vitally important to the war effort that he made us stand, watch, and wait before loading and departure could proceed? Why, his own personal bar of soap-on-a-rope. No, I'm not making this up. There were a hundred witnesses to this performance. When he'd found it and flounced away, not at all embarrassed, without a word of explanation, apology, or even a joke, like a princeling in a snit, and sure as hell without helping to reload the bags, people just shook their heads. And we asked each other: What's in that soap? Cocaine? Diamonds? Cyanide? And then we asked: What if it was really only the soap he was after? Contraband would have made some sort of sense. But what if he'd made us all stand there like that simply because he couldn't be separated for the length of the flight from his little luxury personal grooming item? And this guy's an *officer,* someone whose judgment and savvy we're supposed to entrust our lives and safety to?

Some of the enlisted personnel I'd met in the muster area in Kuwait had not exactly filled me with confidence, either. I recall looking into the eyes of a young woman named Lynddie England. I saw a sort of dazed look that told me she didn't really know where she was or why. If I'd handed her a map and asked her to point to what part of the world we were in at that moment, I believe she would have been helpless. That was the "where;" never mind the "why." She could hardly be blamed for any of it, though, especially that last part. That "why" was a slippery question for everybody, from the lowliest grunts to the four-star generals, and, as it would turn out, for me.

I would come to know Col. Maloney well in the months to follow. Thinking about the soap-on-a-rope business now, I tend to think there was nothing hidden inside it. Sometimes a bar of soap is just a bar of soap, and what we saw that day was merely a display of petty, self-serving vanity. It would not be the last such display.

Speaking of displays, my superior officer was not the only person I'd be working with who didn't mind making other people's lives a little bit harder than they had to be, just for self-entertainment. One of the members of my team, May Ling (not her real name), was a pretty, petite young Chinese-American intelligence officer. On one of our first nights in camp in Kuwait, she demanded "equal treatment" by insisting on sleeping in the bunk tent among the male soldiers. She raised a big ruckus, with threats to cite people for gender discrimination if she didn't get her way.

She got her way and bedded down among at least twenty men; then, during the night, she pleasured herself with audible sighs and moans. Keep in mind that the average age of the men around her was maybe twenty-two. Think anybody got any sleep? The poor SOBs were driven practically insane. Tempers were short the next day, guys imagining rivalries, giving each other dirty looks while many hungry eyes followed May as she went blithely about with demure little dimples on her face as if she were Snow White. Talk about bad for morale. I got the feeling her main reason for joining the military was to put herself in the midst of hundreds of horny young men and toy with them. And she was going to be one of my colleagues in the gathering of vital intelligence? Between her and Maloney, things were off to a splendid start.

———

If the night reveals the war machine, the day reveals the alien planet that is the desert. When I first arrived, I noticed myself feeling lousy in a non-specific sort of way, as if someone had turned up the gravity knob and thickened my blood. Sleep was heavy and sodden, my dreams murky. It wasn't until I saw a thermometer reading 118 degrees in the late morning that I understood why. Most of us have experienced extreme heat, but when you get into the upper teens and are pushing 120, it's a whole different realm. You don't feel it as hotter so much as weightier, duller, a free-floating malaise permeating mind and body. And this was only March. How would it be in June? July?

Of course, you adapt, as had the people and animals who've lived there for generations. I'd made a friend; a lean and hungry feral dog had started appearing on the outskirts of camp, scouting for scraps. Dogs are not exactly pampered in the Muslim world. They're seen as dirty, impure, disease-carrying vermin. This wasn't always so. It's said that the Prophet himself kept dogs, and that for centuries before and after the Prophet they were part of everyday life, put to work doing what dogs do for humans—guarding, herding, protecting, assisting with the hunt, and no doubt providing companionship, too. As cities grew and human populations got denser, dogs came to serve as garbage-eaters.

Sometime a couple of hundred years ago, major contagions swept through the crowded cities, and people thought they saw a correlation between dogs, garbage, and disease, and dogs became the outcasts in many Muslim societies that they are today. You see them everywhere in Iraq and Kuwait—skinny, foraging, wild, sick, mangy, and ignored. It's sad for a bleeding-heart dog-lover like me, but for a while I was able to make life a little more pleasant for my friend who came sniffing around Camp Virginia. I even named him: Rudi the Desert Dog. He found my MREs (ready-to-eat meals) to be quite to his liking. He was particularly fond of the tuna casserole. I figured he liked it so much because the US military version of it reminded Rudi of the roadkill he surely dined upon regularly.

One day, I thought I'd offer him a real treat: a pan of fresh water. I set it out, then sat back to watch what would surely be a joyous moment for Rudi, who looked thirsty all the time. He approached, sniffed, looked at me, plainly saying: You're kidding, right? And he put his nose under the pan and flipped it.

At first, I thought: My God, this desert dog has never experienced water as *water*. He's so thoroughly adapted to this Mars-like environment that whatever moisture he needs to sustain life he gets from food. But another thought occurred to me: the water Rudi had so eloquently disdained was the "purified" stuff provided to the US military by a private contracting company. Private contractors, a polite term for "mercenaries," were enjoying a veritable feeding frenzy with this invasion, swarming in ahead of and alongside the military, raking in huge bucks providing everything from food to security to construction to entertainment to transportation. And, of course, drinking water.

I'd noticed the aroma of chlorine myself in the water; imagine what that would have smelled like to Rudi's nose, a thousand times more sensitive than mine. I might as well have offered him a bowl of Clorox. We all drank this water, because it was that or go thirsty. A little chlorine is tolerated by the human body; too much can have a nasty effect on the kidneys, liver, nervous system, and more. And what else, I wondered, was in that water that I couldn't smell, but Rudi could? Did the company providing the "purified" water give a damn? I doubted it.

Where did Rudi go when nature got ferocious? I don't know, but he was a wily survivor. Springtime in Kuwait and Iraq is not exactly April showers and May flowers. Picture instead occasional tempests of howling winds, maybe sixty or seventy miles per hour. Gritty sand blowing horizontally; pelting you without mercy; getting in your eyes, nose, and mouth; coating faces so that you don't recognize your best buddy; turning the world a weird orange color if it's daytime; and making it so that you can barely see your hand at the end of your outstretched arm. Sandstorms started up with decisive suddenness, roared for hours, and then, just as suddenly, ceased.

We'd endured one of these blowouts just a couple of days before my night in the guard tower. The tents had shuddered and flapped, and our faces looked like weird masks if we went outside for even a few minutes, and you had to shout at the top of your lungs over the wind to talk to somebody right next to you. We made our way from tent to latrine by following guide ropes. Sand got into our weapons, vehicle engines, and electrical generators as well as into our teeth, eyes, ears, and noses. Helicopters were grounded; communications got spotty. People caught out in the open got disoriented and wandered around blindly, and inside the tents, miniature dust devils whirled while people struggled to keep the quaking canvas weighted with sandbags. I heard that somebody got the bright idea to park a seventy-five-ton Abrams tank so it would serve as a windscreen. I think inside the tank would have been an ideal place to ride out the storm.

When the storm quit and the world was restored to its usual broiling stillness, Rudi appeared, hungry but unscathed, looking for a nice MRE. Where did he go during the storm? I asked him, but he wasn't telling.

On March 17, George W. Bush issued his High Noon ultimatum to Saddam Hussein and his boys, Uday and Qusay. You have forty-eight hours, he said, to leave the country or else face the wrath of the coalition forces. Nobody expected Saddam to say Oh, okay, and leave, and he didn't.

On March 19, almost exactly forty-eight hours after Bush's squinty-eyed challenge, a monster sandstorm came raging down from the north. This storm made headlines around the world—not just for its ferocity, which was considerable, but for its timing: the very day of Saddam's Bush-imposed deadline. We hunkered down just as we had for the last one, and just like with the last one, operations pretty much came to a halt while the storm shrieked and the canvas rattled. It was not difficult to imagine Saddam dancing an exultant jig, and inside our shuddering tents there were a lot of uneasy jokes about the wrath of Allah.

But like the other storms, this one subsided, and the war machine engaged its inexorable gears. Any day now, my unit, the 223rd Intelligence Brigade, along with countless other units, would be rolling across the border into Iraq.

Soon enough, I knew, I'd never see Rudi again.

# CHAPTER 3

# IDES OF MARCH

In the wee hours of March 23, the day we'd be pushing over the border into Iraq behind the main invading forces, bad news traveled through Camp Virginia and the other camps: an American soldier had just murdered two officers at nearby Camp Pennsylvania. He did it by lifting the flaps of the officers' tents and rolling hand grenades under the cots where the men were sleeping. The soldier who rolled the grenades was a Muslim convert. And so began an already fraught D-Day.

Soon I was behind the wheel of one of a long, long line of decrepit unarmored Humvees, with a top speed of forty miles per hour, when we crossed the border into Iraq on Highway 8. It was like driving a big heavy old farm truck stuck in low gear. It jounced, whined, and growled along. And without the protection of armor plating, we might just as well have been in an old farm truck. I guess we were supposed to take comfort in the knowledge that we'd be greeted as "liberators." They'll be throwing flowers, we'd been told.

These rusty, creaky, groaning Humvees were actually old acquaintances of mine. I'd seen them before, on the other side of the world, and driven them, had quite possibly driven the very one I was lumbering along in now. And I'd thought at the time: *I pity the fool who has to go to war in one of these hunks of junk.* And now, here I was, going off to war in one of those hunks of junk.

The last time I'd seen these Hummers, they were rusting away in the salt air of Marin County in northern California. Marin County, you say? Isn't that about as far, in every sense, from the deserts of Iraq and Kuwait as you can get? Indeed. And there was more than a little irony around the fact that I was riding in an unarmored vehicle.

Some history: by the time I was driving that clunker over the border, I was hardly a fresh-faced kid—by then, my military career stretched back almost thirty years. I was a trained intelligence agent and analyst, a combat engineer and was halfway through medical school. I was older than the enlisted troops around me by a full generation. When I first joined the military, decades before, I was a raw teenage recruit just like so many of the ones who made up the "boots on the ground" part of this 2003 invasion. When I came of age, the Vietnam war was not quite over, and the draft was still vacuuming up young men. At barely eighteen, instead of waiting around for them to snare me and ship me off to that green hell of death—or running to Canada—I signed up, under my own volition, with the Coast Guard, and avoided actually going to Vietnam, but technically, I'm a Vietnam-era vet.

Rewind further to my childhood: I might be the only person you know who was put in an orphanage as a newborn in mid-1950s California, but later "adopted" by his own biological mother, who'd spent her pregnancy in a home for unwed mothers. I was the issue of a hit-and-run fling between my teenaged mother and an older man, a Korean War vet, whose identity I'd eventually learn. I'd also learn that my biological father was Native American on *his* father's side, a descendant of one of many children born to my paternal great-grandmother who came from Scotland, migrated west to Oklahoma in the late 1800s, and married Chief Black Fox, a Cherokee.

Back to my mother's side of the family: My grandmother, my mother's mother, got me out of the orphanage when I was an infant; then, when my mother found a husband, she gave me back to her. I was about three by then. The guy she married brought hell into my young life. It was the classic heartless prick stepfather syndrome. Here's just one example: I was sitting at the table, eating, when a huge meaty hand came out of nowhere and walloped the side of my head, stunning me and knocking me out of my chair. Why? Because he didn't like the way I was chewing. I was maybe six or seven. I lived in terror of this man for ten years. And I'm sorry to report that my mother never intervened, never tried to protect me.

When I was about thirteen, and my mother's marriage to my stepfather was finally rotted out, and my home life was in violent, drunken chaos, I went to live on a ranch in Plumas County in the Sierra. My unofficial adoptive parents, family friends named Homer and Irene, were Native American, had five boys of their own, and were as kindly to me as my stepfather had been cruel. It had been my idea that I go live with them, and they readily agreed. So did my mother, seeing a chance to be rid of me. Homer and Irene were Yana people, a California tribe closely related to the Yahi, the tribe of Ishi, the famous "last wild Indian" whose poignant story you can read about in the book *ISHI in Two Worlds.*

I was big for my age, and living on a ranch meant hard work, starting before dawn. We were at a high elevation, meaning serious snow in the winter. There were animals to feed and care for year round. There was routine, and there was stability. I thrived on the responsibility and the work, did not mind it at all because of the kindness and fairness. My nervous system healed; there was no screaming, cursing, or bellowing, no kicks, blows, or punches, no ambushes out of the blue, and no toxic threat of danger constantly poisoning the atmosphere.

We worked hard, but we had a lot of fun, too. I learned some rodeo riding, and I learned about compassion for its own sake; the family rescued a fawn, wounded by coyotes, that had come into the corral. We kept the fawn until he became a huge buck and went on his way. My love of animals grew strong on the ranch; even though the cattle were ultimately going to be shipped off to slaughter, they were treated humanely during their lives. And we had a big population of dogs and cats, also fed, loved, and cared for, though we lost a lot of them to the cougars and coyotes.

When I think of Homer, I think of Ben Cartwright—big, wise, solid, benevolent, and good-humored. I know it all sounds impossibly hokey, like a made-up story out of an orphan's fantasy or an over-earnest piece of boys' fiction. But it was real, and I believe Homer and Irene saved me from a sordid fate. Because of them, I avoided the sorry syndrome we see too often: abused kids growing up to be abusers themselves. My time with them taught me about other ways to live, and I made a conscious decision to *not* replicate my stepfather's vile behavior: to avoid, as best I could, ever inflicting that kind of pain, and just as important, to not stand uselessly by like my mother while it was inflicted. I knew what it was like to be trapped, overpowered, and at the mercy of a sadist, and this knowledge would figure crucially decades later in my life.

My mother, meantime, found a second no-good husband, though he was not quite as bad as the first. But I'm grateful for a vital life connection I made through him. He had a friend—a Norwegian explorer named Odd Bjerke, in his sixties by then—who'd been all over the world, from the Amazon to the Arctic. As a youth, he'd known the great Polar explorer Roald Amundsen. Odd invited me to come on an expedition to the Northwest Territories, to the Great Slave Lake in Canada, to do a wildlife survey for the National Geographic. I was fifteen that summer, would turn sixteen in the fall—the perfect age for such a wild and wooly adventure.

And wild it was. He brought along his New York socialite girlfriend, who was more than game, a lot of fun, and freshly broken up with her last squeeze, a fellow by the name of Joe Namath. One of our supply canoes was filled with half-gallon plastic jugs of whiskey. Yes, I learned about wilderness and survival, saw animals galore, including giant brown bears and polar bears, and bathed in icy lakes, but it was Odd's stories of his life, told when he was warmed by whiskey and the campfire, that really opened my young eyes. Not only had he been everywhere in the world, but he'd also been a spy against the Nazis in World War II, had been shot and left for dead by the Germans more than once, and had a chest and belly full of bullet scars (he was happy to pull up his shirt and show us) to prove it. Wanderlust stirred in me, along with a brand-new fascination: the spy business.

When the survey was over, we arrived at the town of Yellowknife, and people went their separate ways. There was no drinking age up there at the time, so I went to a bar one night and had a beer. I met a German guy there, a miner and engineer, who told me I should stay, live at the local firehouse, go to school there in Yellowknife, and come to work in the goldmine.

I decided right then and there to do it. How many teenage kids get a chance to make a life decision like that, over a beer, a couple of thousand miles from home? Certainly not many in today's "helicopter parent" environment. I stayed. I went to school (junior year) in the morning and then rode the bucket down into the hard rock mine. I learned about the engineering, chemistry, and physics of gold mining, saw the labor-intensity of it, the tons and tons of rock blasted, moved, and crushed to produce a single brick of gold. And I was getting paid, earning my own way, being my own man, and getting a fine education both above the ground in the school and below in the mine. I occasionally joined Native Canadian firefighting crews, battling tundra fires, and got to know people who seemed like long-lost cousins.

After about ten months, I went back to California. My seventeenth birthday was coming up that fall. Much as I loved Homer and Irene and the ranch, I quickly knew I'd outgrown that life. The near year away had transformed me. Half the miners I rubbed shoulders with had been European, and there were expat Americans dodging the draft and Vietnam, plus a music and cultural scene that was all new and mind-blowing to me. Thanks to the first-rate high school I'd attended, with its British-based system and curriculum, so superior to my American school, I learned about real education and its rewards, and learned that I loved to learn.

Our little local high school there in Plumas County now looked pathetically rinky-dink, my classmates like naïve grade-schoolers. No way, after Canada, the wilderness, the mine, the firefighting, and the school, was I going to plod through my senior year there. I was spring-loaded and itching to get out into the big world. So I pushed hard, got my GED equivalency, graduated early, and was off to Chico State at the age of seventeen, where I began a combined major in anthropology/archaeology, and on the side, did some actual rodeo riding. I'm here to say I rode some of the biggest, baddest bulls on the local rodeo circuit, and was lucky not to have broken my neck. I even remember their names: Hippie, Half Breed, and Tombstone . . .

I met a couple of guys at Chico, Vietnam vets. I noticed they were getting nice green government checks in the mail every month, while I was working laying irrigation pipes in orchards. The war was still grinding on, the draft lottery sowing killer suspense. My next birthday would be my eighteenth, when I'd have to register. I sure as hell didn't want to go to Vietnam, but the idea of joining the military and getting my education paid for, and getting some of those nifty checks myself on a regular basis, was tantalizing. Mainly, though, it was education I wanted: I was starting to entertain the idea of studying medicine. And so I signed up with the Coast Guard the minute I was old enough. That was how I dodged a possible ticket to death in the jungle.

My first assignment was presidential security, guarding the sea approach to Richard Nixon's Western White House in San Clemente, our armed Coast Guard cutter anchored forty-five yards from shore when Nixon was in residence. This was late 1972. Watergate was already coming down by then, and unfolded inexorably over the next couple of years. I was in a unique position to closely follow the cascade of events, right up to Nixon's resignation in August of 1974. This was a crash course for me—still a baby in a lot of ways—in politics, societal and governmental dynamics, and the effects of power. I was, as they say, getting "politicized." Though my studies in anthropology were incomplete, what I'd learned about evolution and hierarchy became a little more three-dimensional as I witnessed the Nixon saga from my front row seat. I was getting to know the human animal more and more intimately.

And that knowledge would deepen. After Nixon flew into the sunset in his helicopter, the Coast Guard sent me across the country, to New London, Connecticut, to the Hospital Corpsman "A" School. A Medical Corpsman is a rigorously trained technician, ready and able to take care of the medical needs of everyone on a boat or a base where there's no nearby doctor or hospital. I thought I knew a thing or two about studying and academics, but I might as well have come to that school from kindergarten. This six-month course was an absolute no-fooling-around ass-buster. The curriculum was a compressed form of the first two years of medical school. So I shifted into high gear, graduated, and it was on to the next adventure.

This one felt like a real reward: a month aboard the US Coast Guard Cutter Eagle. The Eagle is a full-on three-masted sailing ship, a total beauty surrendered by the Germans after WWII as part of war reparations. On board this magnificent, tall ship, cadets learn seamanship, navigation, and teamwork. I learned all of that, plus the meaning of true exhilaration. Unless you've experienced it, you can't imagine how it is to feel the timeless power of wind and sails and kinship with sailors down through the centuries.

After that, it was two years on a 210-foot Coast Guard cruiser, chasing drug smugglers around the Caribbean and down to South America. We also made regular stops at Cay Sal Bank, a tiny island between Cuba and Florida, to look for and rescue refugees from Cuba. Cay Sal had been a CIA training ground as well. Oil rigs stood just off Cay Sal. Guess who they belonged to? None other than George H. W. Bush, director of the CIA from 1976 to 1977. Helicopters regularly serviced those platforms, and rumor had it that those helicopters, immune to inspection, often flew back to the United States loaded with cocaine brought in from South America on fishing boats. This was my first "close encounter" with GHWB, but it would not be my last.

We were headquartered in South Florida. One evening at a bar in Key West, I got into a chat with a small, dapper, hard-drinking, dark-haired and mustachioed older fellow. He was kindly, a dazzling conversationalist, and mentioned that he'd written some plays. I'd heard of one of them, because it had been made into a movie starring Elizabeth Taylor: *Cat on a Hot Tin Roof.* As the day waned, we went outside, drinks in hand, to join the hundreds of Key Westers who convened every night to toast the sunset. In the slanting golden rays of the sinking sun, we met a guy with an iguana on each of his shoulders; the critters were dressed in tiny little iridescent sequined vests and wearing miniature fezzes on their heads. They walked slowly and thoughtfully along the man's arms. I bade them all farewell and was on my way. That was the first and last time I'd talk to Tennessee Williams.

After the Coast Guard, I joined the Navy. I was a medical corpsman for the Navy Seals and for the Marine Force Recon commandos. This took me to around 1982, when I was recruited by Army Intelligence. This was when I first went to intelligence school, in Boston, to study electronic surveillance: intercepts, jamming, sweeping for listening devices—everything you associate with spying. Then it was back to California to another spy school, in Los Alamitos, where I studied intelligence analysis—what you do with the information you've gathered. For the next decade or so, I travelled, on assignment, running operations everywhere from Asia to Europe to South America.

From the Army I went into the California National Guard. I was still in the military, but in the Reserves now, which meant I could take a civilian job. I chose one where the pay was high, there was generous vacation time, and where my training and experience would serve me well: Corrections Officer at Folsom Prison, where, in addition to other duties, I was in charge of the intelligence data base to be used in developing what was called the Violence Management Plan for combatting gang warfare within prisons. That work involved surveillance and analysis, two of my specialties. Knowing something about anthropology didn't hurt, either. I actually testified before the California State Senate about the efficacy of this program.

I met some celebrities at Folsom, including Rick James, the Menendez brothers, Kenneth Bianchi (a.k.a. the Hillside Strangler), and Charles Manson. Take it from me: Charlie was a lot less impressive in person than he was on that famous LIFE magazine cover. Don't tell anyone, but I actually saved his life in a SHU (Secure Housing Unit)-yard brawl one day. A massive Aryan Nation brute by the name of Cornfed was on top of the 5'2" Charlie, strangling him with his two huge hands. The fight had something to do with a Manson "girl" on the outside. Charlie's face was turning purple. I pulled my revolver and took aim at Charlie and Cornfed. I had a clear shot at either. I moved my sight from one to the other; here was my chance to go down in history as the man who killed Charles Manson. *Do I? Don't I? Do I?* In the end, restraint prevailed. I moved the sight just so, shot Cornfed in the hip, blasting him clean off Charlie, who would live for nearly another thirty years.

Then, with the first Gulf War, late 1990 to early 1991, I'd be activated to brief personnel going to the Middle East to fight. By that time in my career, I was not only a school-educated intelligence analyst and electronic counterintelligence specialist, I was also a specialist in desert warfare, which meant analyzing the desert battlefield, with emphasis on armor and air power and the critical ways the two were essential to winning in such an environment.

Saddam had put on a hell of a show with his bluster and blarney about "the Mother of all wars," and he managed to actually scare a lot of people into believing he was in possession of a doomsday arsenal. But part of my job was to find out exactly what Saddam really had in the way of weapons, troops, armor, and support—what kind of capabilities the coalition units would actually be facing—and educate them about those particulars. So I was in a unique position to know a thing or two about armor by the time I was at the wheel of that Humvee.

Most of us, when we think "armor," think simply of a thick slab of metal, with rocks, arrows, or bullets bouncing off it, and that's what armor pretty much was, from the time humans and metal discovered one another. But modern armor is way more sophisticated and complex than that, and has evolved as weaponry has evolved, becoming weaponized itself. We knew that the Russian tanks being used by the Iraqis, for example, were equipped with what's called "active armor." Invented by the Russians not long after WWII, it's basically a layer of high explosive sandwiched between metal plates. The idea is that when an anti-tank projectile hits that armor, it's met by a counter-explosion, forcing the metal plates apart and damaging or deflecting the attacking projectile. And it works damned well. There are plenty of varieties, the technology highly complex, with a great range of effects, and it was my job to know all of it. On our side, we had space-age armor that was the stuff of science fiction. And of course, the more formidably science-fictionish our armor became, the more the Russians—the main supplier to whoever our enemy might be—invented devilishly strange anti-tank weaponry that you'd swear had been beamed down by the Klingons. Later, during my time in Iraq in '03, I'd see the effects of some of these otherworldly weapons and ask myself if perhaps we were in an interstellar war and just didn't know it yet.

But I'm getting ahead of myself.

By the year 1999, I was recruited by the 250th Military Intelligence unit in Marin County to become a full-fledged intelligence agent, and I would be sent off to a special school in Arizona to get my badge and credentials. September 11 and the cascade of repercussions that would follow had not yet happened. You may recall that within a month of 9/11 we officially invaded Afghanistan, but the truth is we were already in there. We had been for years, under the guise of "special operations," part of a tangle of shifting alliances and covert operations involving international oil pipelines and mining and mineral interests—and later, efforts to assassinate bin Laden after the bombing of US embassies in Kenya and Tanzania and to prop up the Northern Alliance against the Taliban, thought to be shielding bin Laden. With 9/11, we would pour into Afghanistan like Attila the Hun's army, covert no more.

And the war in Iraq, which would not officially begin until the 2003 invasion, had been for quite some time way more than just a gleam in the neocon eye. Much later, long after I was out of Iraq and bringing legal charges against various of my cohort and commanders, I would learn that as of the inauguration of George W. Bush in 2000 there was a deeply entrenched, unstoppable, and highly illegal intent in place to invade Iraq, and that this intent was euphemistically called "pre-planned aggression." Bush and Cheney and the gang were slavering for an opportunity to set the plan into motion. The First Gulf War had only whetted their appetites; the truth is that they simply hadn't made enough money during that earlier go-round. Here was their chance to rectify that wrong. With some deeply cynical sleight of hand and masterful propaganda, they shifted blame for 9/11 to Saddam and Iraq, and vast portions of the public eagerly bought into it. A year and a half after 9/11, the invasion was underway.

When I began my course to get my badge and credentials, I could not have known how it would all consummate three years hence, and I didn't know then the extent of this "pre-planned aggression," but I did know Iraq was in the air again, and my expertise included Iraq—history, customs, and what they had and didn't have in the way of forces and weapons. I had no reason then to think that I myself would be sent over there; I believed that if there were another incursion into Iraq that I would be doing similar work to what I did during the First Gulf War: briefing, training, and advising. I assumed I'd also possibly be briefing people being dispatched to Afghanistan.

How, you might ask, could I participate in any way in these ill-advised, illegal, money-grubbing wars? This is a good place for me to put forth my philosophy, which is similar to that of T. E. Lawrence (of Arabia): if there must be a war, then cause as little bloodshed as possible. "Force protection" was my specialty; I believed that I could save lives with what I knew about that part of the world and what they had in the way of armaments. I believed that my abilities as a trained intelligence agent, along with my other skills, could be an effective diplomatic tool as well as a way to keep death and destruction to a minimum for everybody.

There were a lot of different kinds of intelligence that could be collected to that end, aside from military intelligence. There was, for example, civilian economic intelligence. This was another way of saying: knowing who the local leadership was, who could be bribed and who couldn't, who could be recruited and who couldn't—and how these various people related to one another, all of it requiring a personal touch, patience, flexibility, trustworthiness, and cultural sensitivity. To my mind, this was every bit as important as knowing what sort of weaponry we'd be up against. That was vital to know, too, of course, and I was already a qualified specialist in explosives as well as armor. I knew just about everything there was to know about different types of mines. I could build them and take them apart. I'd studied the Iraqi army, knew that in structure and sheer rigor it was a lot like both the Soviet army and the North Korean army: in other words, iron discipline and a sort of hive-like cohesiveness that made our own modern military look rag-tag by comparison.

That cohesiveness included a fierce willingness to die. The battle cry of such armies, where the individual soldier's identity is subsumed and he becomes a living component of a larger organism (think army ants, forming a bridge over a stream so other ants can cross), might go something like this: Ten thousand might die, but there are twenty-five thousand right behind them.

The training I'd get in qualifying for my badge and credentials would enhance what I already knew as an intelligence analyst and make me an official intelligence agent. So, in the year 2000, under the auspices of the 250th

Intelligence Unit, off I went to agent school in Arizona, at Ft. Huachuca. It was a fascinating, intense, in-depth course of study.

Sometimes an event is unusual and compelling in and of itself, and sometimes it becomes downright enthralling in retrospect. In July of 2000, while I was at Ft. Huachuca, we were paid a visit by one Col. Anthony Shaffer, an intelligence agent, and two other members of the team of agents he'd been working with in an intensive military counterterrorism operation known as Able Danger. A group of about thirty-five of us convened in a secured Quonset hut, that homely-but-practical circa WWII prefab shelter ubiquitous to military installations. Shaffer and his guys were present in the Quonset with us.

"Col. Shaffer has briefed me," said our class commander. "And now I am briefing you. Sometime in the next eighteen months, New York City and Washington, DC will be attacked. Civilian airliners will be hijacked and flown into the World Trade Center and selected targets in DC."

Yes, he said that. A data-mining program used by Able Danger had determined that there were at least two cells of "terrorist operatives" inside the United States at that moment: that those cells had been "penetrated" by Able Danger operatives, that members of these terrorist cells had received flight training in south Florida and at an old abandoned air base not far from where we were in Arizona, and that their leader was Osama bin Laden.

And he told us that we should get our affairs in order, settle our debts, and make out our wills, because when these attacks occurred we would be "activated" to hunt down Al Qaeda terrorists and would be going to the Middle East. During the Q and A that followed, someone in our group asked which official domestic agencies had been told about what we'd just been told, since military intelligence can't legally operate inside the country due to Posse Comitatus laws, which restrict the use of the military in enforcing domestic laws.

"The NSA, the CIA, and the FBI," one of the Able Danger guys answered.

Someone else in the class asked the obvious question: "If we know who they are and where they are and what they're planning, why don't we just pick them up?"

"Because they haven't done anything yet. So far, they're just foreign nationals who've been taking flying lessons."

When the meeting was over, the Quonset hut was destroyed. For security, just in case it had been bugged. This was routine. All that was left of this Quonset and the many others razed—testament to numerous top-secret confabulations—was a rectangular cement base, studded with turquoise. We were, after all, in the Southwest.

After 9/11, Shaffer would claim that more than a year before the attacks Able Danger had briefed the CIA and other agencies about the terrorist cells inside the United States, and that those agencies hadn't acted on the information, but he would then claim that Able Danger had *not* briefed the FBI. That last claim contradicted what we'd been told at the secret meeting, and in retrospect, seems to be a falsehood designed to give cover to the government for not preventing the attacks. Curiouser and curiouser.

But of course, we did not have crystal balls that day in July of 2000, and could not have known any of that nor the stunning implications.

When my course of study at agent school was done, I learned that I was one of only five such credentialed intelligence agents for the Department of Defense with expertise specific to Southwest Asia.

In 2001, I transferred from the 250th in Marin to the 223rd in Sacramento, fondly referred to by some as the "dog pit" unit. My commander at the 250th took me aside and begged me not to transfer. Others warned me. *Don't do it*, they said. *That unit's nothing but trouble.* But I was determined to make the transfer so I could be at home in Sacramento. And I thought: *How bad could it be?*

I got a taste pretty quickly. When I arrived, the Battalion Commander, one Col. Craig Maloney, was in the process of firing the Company Commander. The guy being fired, an airline pilot, was deeply pissed at the way it was going down. There was an atmosphere of grumbling, grousing, resentment, and back-stabbing—just general bad vibes. The pilot's parting words to me, the new arrival, as he walked out the door were not uplifting: Good luck with this unit. You're gonna need it.

In the meantime, as if I didn't have enough to do, I decided to go for my medical degree. I needed to find a medical school that could accommodate my work and military obligations, so I enrolled in Oceania University of Medicine, based in Samoa, which specializes in serving students like me—older and leading full lives of work and obligations but who are determined to become doctors. The course of study was partly online and partly hands-on and in person. When I had vacation time from Folsom and was not on military assignment, I'd fly off to Samoa. And I had a great head start: that six-month Hospital Corpsman course I'd taken years before in Connecticut counted, credit-wise, as my first two years of medical school. It would be a haul, I knew, but if I paced myself, I could quite possibly be an MD when I retired from the military.

---

A little after 6:30 a.m. on September 11, 2001, after I'd been with the 223rd for a few months, I was on my way to open the unit, my first time at being first through the door.

I was still in the car when a call came in from Kathy, my partner and sweetie.

"The Pentagon's been attacked," she said. "And so has the World Trade Center in New York."

Some people getting similar calls on that morning recall thinking for a few moments that maybe there was some leg-pulling going on. I didn't, though. First, Kathy would never perpetrate a "joke" like that, and second, I'd been told, fourteen months earlier, that this would happen

*Jesus,* I thought, *Shaffer totally nailed it.*

Like most of the world, as soon as I reached a TV—in my case, at the 223rd headquarters—I flipped it on. Both towers had already been hit, the North Tower first, I learned, and then, less than twenty minutes later, the South Tower, when a second plane came hurtling in with deadly aim. That was the moment when the world understood that what we were seeing was not some freak accident, like the time in 1945 when an American bomber plane hit the Empire State Building in heavy fog. There was no fog over New York on September 11. Black smoke billowed from the towers into a flawless razor-blue sky. That's what so many of us remember—the serene beauty of the day as the backdrop to smoke, fire, chaos, cataclysm, mass confusion, and desperate people jumping to their deaths. You could see birds in the distance in that perfect sky, going about their business, not overly perturbed by the human kerfuffle below.

I barely had time to get a grip on what I was seeing when the South Tower accordioned to the ground, in an almost languid sort of way, to the accompaniment of thousands of people screaming at the sight, just under an hour after the second plane hit. That was when it was brought home to me, and to everyone else watching, that something enormous was afoot, that I was witnessing a historic moment equivalent to Pearl Harbor. As the years went by, I would learn much more about the extent of that enormity; for now, though, like everyone else, I knew my life would never be quite the same. When the North Tower went down less than a half hour later, I knew this for a certainty.

What I couldn't have known was that, in fact, my life would be turned upside down, inside out, and sideways, to the point where I hardly recognized it as my life.

How and when would I and my fellow intel agents be "activated," as Shaffer had said we would? About a year after the Americans' swift invasion of Afghanistan in the month following 9/11, and after the failure to catch Bin Laden despite the braggadocio of Bush & Co. that we'd "bomb it into a parking lot," I was called into what we kiddingly referred to as the "Dome of Silence" after the old '60s spy spoof TV show *Get Smart*. It was actually a small soundproof un-bugged room at the 223rd headquarters.

There were four other people in the room aside from me. One of them was a certain 1st Sgt. Padilla (not his real name) (a.k.a. "Sgt. Gorilla") and another was a guy I knew, a warrant officer at the San Francisco unit of the 223rd, under whom Padilla worked. This warrant officer also happened to be Kathy's cousin, though this was not general knowledge.

Sgt. Padilla had a big surprise for me after he swore me in for this secret huddle. He told me my badge and credentials would be going into a top-secret vault in Arizona. Then he announced that there would be a "briefing" on Iraq. When I heard the word "briefing," I immediately thought I would be the one giving it, since that had been my job before. But it turned out that this time, I'd be the one being briefed, by an officer from another command.

The major who came to give us our briefing was a great big gal in uniform. She had the smile, gloss, and gleam of an inspirational infomercial speaker with a product to sell.

"Guess what?" she said, beaming around the room as if she were about to tell us we'd won an all-expenses-paid trip to Aruba. "We're going to Iraq!" She looked way too happy when she said it.

That was a rhetorical "we." She, in fact, was not going to Iraq. But the rest of us in the 223rd Intelligence Brigade, including me, were. And I was told that my know-how, especially in the area of IPB—Intelligence Preparation of the Battlefield—was one of the main reasons I was quite literally being conscripted. On top of that, I'd be the unit's medic.

I had expected to be called upon if the attack materialized, as Shaffer had said we would, and sent to the Middle East, but I never thought Iraq would be my destination. Afghanistan, maybe, or Yemen, Pakistan, or Kuwait, but not Iraq. And by now, I was well acquainted with my unit, the 223rd. Let's just say they would not have been my first choice of whom to go with into a battle zone.

This was late 2002. Though I'd known I might be "activated," I'd gone ahead and put in my letter of retirement, just in case. In about another year, September of 2003, I'd be eligible to hang up my cleats after thirty years in the military. If I happened to be "activated" and overseas somewhere, and my retirement date came along, I could possibly leave and go home. My full benefits would kick in. I'd finish medical school. A new world awaited me. But as Bobby Burns sagely reminded us, even the best-laid plans can go awry. I couldn't have known it on that day, but mine were already doing just that.

And so I was given my itinerary: I'd be doing a tour of exactly 364 days, not 365, which would have been a full year. By shaving off a day, they efficiently shaved off any extra retirement benefits they'd have to give me. I was not the only older, seasoned person with multiple skills, close to retirement, getting rounded up this way. You have to admire the ruthless efficiency: with me, they'd be getting an intelligence agent, a combat engineer, and a medic for the bargain price of one. And no promotion for me. Think of the money they saved!

Oh, and get this—I'd be paying for all my clothing, equipment, and even medical supplies out of my own pocket. I wasn't alone, though I was part of an "exclusive" group; this was a special arbitrarily bestowed "privilege" for those of us who were older, held good jobs, and had extensive accomplishment, experience, and credentials under our belts. They knew that we, unlike the young recruits, could afford it, and so they made us pay. Outrageous? I certainly thought so. But tough shit. It ended up costing me about 5K to get exploited. I had zero choice; I'd avoided Vietnam when I was a youth, and now, in the era of the all-volunteer military, I was, for all intents and purposes, a draftee.

This was how it happened that I was old enough to be the father of most of the American troops going into Iraq in 2003.

By early January of 2003, the unit began moving from camp to camp all over the United State, preparing for Iraq, and we were put in what's called "isolation." It wasn't total isolation, but we were pretty much sequestered, cut off from television and newspapers and other outside sources. Plus we were intently focused on the job at hand, like getting ourselves up to speed on all the complex new technologies. We heard rumors about protest marches in the outside world, but that was downplayed. We had no idea that these marches were happening not just in the United States but all over the world, that this was historic, by far the biggest mobilization of protestors in the history of humanity, that millions on every continent were rising up with a huge reverberating NO to Bush and Cheney's war. Our commanders surely knew about this, but there wasn't one word from them about it. Nothing.

And as we now know, none of it amounted to a mouse squeak in a typhoon. Bush is said to have dismissed the marching multi-millions as a "focus group." A monster machine of countless parts had engaged its gears, Dick Cheney in the driver's seat, and was not about to stop because of several million wimps bleating about world peace.

———

And now here I was, in the driver's seat of a machine perfectly symbolic of the waste, haste, and greed of this "preplanned aggression." The last time I saw these raggedy old Humvees was when I was training with the 250th in Marin County before my deployment. There were hundreds of them, a giant fleet, probably built sometime in the '90s, stored there in the open in the Marin salt air, never washed, never maintained, and never driven. They were in miserable shape, in addition to being unarmored. We struggled to get them started so we could train up on driving them. I complained to the motor pool people. "If we ever have to go to war in these things, we're dead meat," I said. They, who would ride out the invasion from the safety of Marin County, bristled: "Don't tell us our business!"

The very same Humvees got loaded onto a ship and sent to Kuwait. And they still hadn't been washed. I remember standing there in the Death Valley-dry desert looking at the encrustations of California salt on those jalopies. I seriously doubted there'd been any mechanical inspection or work, either. Later, I'd learn that there were fleets of well-maintained, armored Humvees, but they were unavailable to us because they were still in Bosnia, and nobody wanted to bother with the paperwork it would take to get them shipped to Kuwait.

During the months leading up to our deployment, I'd had a lot of exposure to both young grunts and officers. Between the truly impressive ignorance of the kids and the arrogance, condescension, and diamond-hard venality of the officers, who appeared to think only of the advancement of their individual careers, some dark doubts had already set up camp in my mind. If you asked the kids what they thought of the state of international diplomacy, they might say: "What's that? A new computer game?" If you mentioned Vietnam, they'd give you a blank, cow-like look. If you listened closely to the murmurings of the officers, you'd hear their steady mantra: *Six-figure salary, six-figure salary!*

And so it came to be that an unarmored Humvee that might break down at any moment and which provided just about zero protection from enemy fire was the chariot I'd be riding into this hot mess.

---

There's not much geographical difference between southern Iraq and northern Kuwait, but it was plain that we were in another country. Not only another country, but one we'd pounded without mercy during the Gulf War of 1991. Grinding our way north toward the little border city of Safwan in our old Humvees became a sort of nightmarish trip down memory lane as burnt, rusted-out vehicles started to appear. They'd been shoved to the side of the road and arranged in piles in a way that suggested a grim miles-long monument to what had happened here a dozen years before.

Photos from that time showed incinerated corpses in the cabs of trucks and cars and on the sand. Marines and GIs on the ground in the aftermath had called them "crispy critters." All of us have been in traffic jams and some of us have imagined how it would be if a disaster of some sort were to occur while we were trapped in our cars and trucks. That's exactly what happened to countless thousands as they fled Iraq-occupied Kuwait, only it was death from above as American planes and Apache helicopters strafed, bombed, and burned. The American public was told that the escapees killed in this operation were all enemy forces, but what I saw were mainly the remains of light civilian pickups, cars, and buses. *Just people*, I thought as we lumbered past on this very same highway. *Just people, trying to get the hell out.*

Some of the hulks were close enough so that we could see the angle of the bullet holes, suggesting low-flying, exuberant cowboy-style strafing. Some of those pilots were obviously having a ball. And we knew that the wreckage we were seeing was red-hot with radiation from the DU (depleted uranium) fortified ammo. The corpses, and all traces of them, were gone by now. I couldn't help but think of Rudi the Desert Dog and his compatriots doing "cleanup." All was quiet now, but the ghastliness and gratuitously cruel overkill lingered. And by then, we knew about the surrendering Iraqi conscripts being buried alive in their trenches during Gulf War 1 by Americans driving armored bulldozers and tanks fitted with earthmoving blades. And we knew about the further cruelty of US-imposed sanctions on Iraq in the years following the war, the economic equivalent of burying defenseless common people in the sand while those at the top, Saddam and his gang, were unaffected.

We had to climb a steep hill to get to Safwan, and my Humvee was not liking it. I radioed Col. Maloney, told him my vehicle was about to overheat, that we should maybe pause to check our radiators. He barked back:

"That's a negative. Keep driving."

"Colonel, this thing could seize up completely."

"Are you deaf? I said *drive*! That's an *order*!"

And so I drove, with the feeling that I'd just earned a special place in Maloney's heart.

As we went, we saw evidence of recent death and destruction. Only a couple of days before, the main invading Coalition forces, led by the Americans, had wiped out a pocket of Iraqi resistance right near the little city. A fearsome barrage of US military might had ended in a sky-high fireball and many Iraqi deaths.

The stopping and starting was like an endless rush hour in hell, and I kept an anxious eye on the temperature gauge. At this point, we were traveling alongside a British convoy. We were halted, engines idling hotly, when I glanced to my right. Next to my Humvee, and a little ahead so that I was looking at its rear door, was a Land Rover personnel vehicle, the Brit version of a Humvee. The door opened, and out popped a tall, pretty, blonde female soldier. As she slapped dust from her derriere, she looked right at me with a radiant smile and said in her charming accent: "I've got a dirty bum!" Behind her, the Land Rover door swung slowly all the way open.

Inside, two husky male soldiers were hard at work beating a skinny little Arab man as if they meant to pound his skull through the metal floor. The man was not moving; he looked possibly dead already. The blonde, walking about stretching her legs, was breezily blasé about the crunch of flesh and bone behind her. She seemed equally unconcerned with me witnessing it. The men doing the beating didn't seem to notice or care, either. Worse, I picked up a definite vibe: they were *enjoying* bludgeoning the guy to a pulp, and didn't give a damn who knew it.

I had no time to ask what or why. Next thing I knew, my line began to crawl, and I had to leave the Brits to their fun.

I wasn't naïve. In my years in Corrections at Folsom, I'd seen violence worse than this, and I knew human nature a little too well. But wasn't this supposed to be "Operation Iraqi Freedom?" I looked in the rear view mirror. *Should I sound the alarm? We're going into a country to supposedly liberate them and we're beating people to death?*

I was in a bad bind. Though our closest allies and part of the Coalition, those were Brits, not Americans, and we were under strict orders: Do *not* interfere with another country's human rights issues. At the same time, I, a medic all my adult life and now halfway through medical school, had internalized the caveat within the Hippocratic Oath: first, do no harm.

Deeply conflicted, I drove on.

That night, we pulled over to sleep. I parked my Humvee so that there was plenty of space between my vehicle and the next. We were totally exposed out there, proverbial sitting ducks, and I was thinking of safety and escape in the event of an attack.

Next thing I knew, Col. Maloney was striding over.

"What the hell are you doing, Ford? Close that gap. NOW!"

Pissed and exasperated, but not in the mood to argue, I closed the gap. But that didn't mean I was willing to be trapped in a surprise ambush. I went up to the roof of the Humvee, spread out my sleeping bag, lay down, and prepared to spend my first night in Iraq.

Sleep was a long time coming. I lay on my back and looked up at the infinite black desert sky, the stars, meteor showers, and countless crisscrossing satellites almost blinding in their brilliance and clarity.

# CHAPTER 4

# THE SWORD AND
# THE CRESCENT

Picture this: a camel with two men on its back materializing, shimmering and mirage-like, out of swirling wind and sand. Just a silhouette at first, moving with that timeless ponderous camel gait, as if from another century, then coming into focus and full physical reality just a few feet from us. Fierce black eyes regarded us over the checkered *keffiyah* on the men's heads and wrapped around their noses and mouths. The camel's huge hairy sides heaved. We did not exactly reach for our weapons, but we were wary and attentive. They looked at us, we looked at them.

We had rolled north at dawn that morning. We'd seen more Highway of Death detritus, and more evidence of posts of Iraqi resistance annihilated. The Highway of Death wreckage gradually petered out; it was plain that the fleeing multitudes had not made it very far before they felt the full force of American might.

The weather can change in the blink of an eye at this time of year in southern Iraq. This day had started clear and calm, but then the wind picked up in an ominous way. Soon the sun faded out and the atmosphere began to change to a Martian sort of color. A familiar moaning sounded. Sandstorm!

We happened to be near a Navy Weather Station. We stopped and prepared to hunker down. I made my way to the Navy Station to see about stocking up on medical supplies. By the time I was on my way back to the convoy, I could see only a few feet in front of me. It's one thing to be in a sandstorm while you're in the relative security of camp on the other side of the border; it's quite another to be a good forty or fifty miles over that border as part of a military procession which, depending on the particular eyes watching, might be perceived as either friend or enemy. It's an insecure feeling, to put it mildly, to not be able to see who or what might be out there. That's how it was for us as the sandstorm closed around us and the men on the camel appeared.

One of them greeted us in Arabic. As soon as he spoke, we could hear the youth in his voice. Up on the camel, with his face wrapped, he could have been a forty-year-old man, some sort of scary hardcore mujahedeen terrorist, but now we saw that he was a boy of perhaps sixteen or seventeen. Our interpreter was close by, so we called him over.

They were brothers. And they had an offer for the Americans.

"Some of Saddam's soldiers are not so far away," one of them said through the interpreter. "They are only about one hundred and fifty yards in that direction." He pointed. "There are just a few of them. We would be pleased to go and kill them for you, cut off their heads, and bring each head to you in a bag made from the scrotum of a camel so that you could carry them with you. We will do this for five dollars per head."

I have to admit this offer made a certain amount of economic sense. What would it cost us in time, money, and resources to go take care of a nest of hostiles? Why not pay these guys five bucks per, and have them do it for us? A little outsourcing.

We declined, of course. Though I was sorry to be turning down such an exotic item for my collection as a tote bag made from a camel's scrotum.

I'm kidding. The encounter with these young men gave us an unsettling firsthand taste of the abiding hatred between Shia and Sunni that had existed for centuries, had been suppressed and contained under Saddam, and was now reemerging, very much alive. Saddam, of course, was Sunni, as were his defenders and fighters. The young men who offered us severed Sunni heads were almost certainly Shia. As the brothers and the camel melted back into the sandstorm and vanished, I reflected that we for sure were not in Kansas anymore. . . .

———

We passed by the city of Basra, close to where the Tigris and Euphrates meet to form one mighty river. Those rivers are literally rivers of life in an otherwise parched landscape, and have been for thousands of years. They made the great civilization of old possible. We passed Nasiriyah; we didn't know it yet, but Jessica Lynch and her 507th Maintenance Company had already made their wrong turn into the city on March 23. They were ambushed; eleven of them were killed, and five, including Lynch, were captured. She'd end up in a Nasiriyah hospital after being held for a while by the Iraqi military regiment that captured her. It doesn't take a great stretch of the imagination to know what that probably meant for the young, pretty, blonde American female soldier. Her eventual rescue happened in spite of an early blunder on the part of the Americans, who, when Iraqi doctors from the hospital tried to return her to them, fired on the ambulance she was being carried in.

About twenty miles south of Baghdad, we came to Al QaQaa, Saddam's world-famous weapons stronghold, eleven square miles of chemical plants, ordnance factories, and underground storage bunkers. It's a huge high-tech violence industrial park, possibly the biggest weapons depot on the planet. Saddam built it in the '70s, with help from the Germans and the Yugoslavians, finishing it just in time for his eight-year, one-million-dead war with Iran. Everything he needed for production and delivery was under one roof, so to speak. Not only were rockets, bombs, and ammunition manufactured there, but there were on-site factories producing centrifuges, aluminum, and steel—all crucial support for the various processes. The reinforced storage bunkers were packed with a full inventory of deadliness.

This place had been heavily bombed during Gulf War 1, but rebuilt in the years after, to the extent that as of 2002, the Brits and the Americans were worried about Saddam whipping up actual nuclear devices there. You may remember the "aluminum tube" business in the run-up to the '03 invasion; these tubes, which had been intercepted being delivered to Al Qa'Qaa, were alleged to be part of Saddam's plan to produce enriched uranium. In the end, though, after UN Weapons inspectors had been all over Al Qa'Qaa at least ten times, it was officially proclaimed that no nuclear WMD were being manufactured or stashed there. The inspectors sealed up the bunkers where explosives were stored and left the country. After the Americans took control of Iraq, those UN inspectors were not allowed back in.

By the time our convoy got there, Al Qa'Qaa had been bombed and ripped apart again by the Americans. We were bewildered at the sight that met our eyes. The place was bustling with activity: civilians swarming everywhere, sacking and looting, and carting armloads of munitions to their casually-parked pickup trucks. It looked like a total free-for-all, the atmosphere almost festive, not a soldier or guard of any sort anywhere in sight. Here was the very facility that had been the center of worldwide controversy, now vanquished and under our control, but left completely unguarded, like a department store with its doors standing open. It made no sense. At least, not then it didn't. Later, the puzzle pieces would fit together with a grim logic that would have made Darth Vader proud: the weapons, ammunition, and explosives being carted away from this all-you-can-carry smorgasbord would spread throughout the population and later be used by the "insurgency" to maim and kill Americans and our allies, justifying our continued occupation.

Does it sound cynical to say that this might have been exactly the plan, a way to stoke the war, keep it going indefinitely and keep Iraq "open for business" by Bush/Cheney-backed giant corporations such as Boeing, Blackwater, Halliburton, Bechtel, Carlyle, and dozens of no-bid private contractors? If you think I'm being ungenerous, stay with me. Again, I'm getting ahead of myself.

We went in. We were completely ignored. No one seemed at all perturbed by our presence. We drove slowly along the unpaved roads wending their way around the part of the facility where the bunkers were. One of these bunkers, its door bulging with pressure from within, caught our attention. We went and took a close look: so great was the pressure from inside that the outer latch could not be budged. Now we were really curious, so we drove our Humvee right up against the door, revved, pushed it in just enough to free the latch. Guess what we found in there? A massive stash of American-made high-speed nuclear deto-nators stacked in wooden crates marked with the familiar international radia-tion-warning symbol known as the "trefoil." The trefoils in front of us were magenta against a yellow background, a color combination used only in the United States. There had been jokes during the search for WMD in the run-up to the war, to the effect that we knew Saddam had them because we had the receipts. The American-made detonators were, as it would turn out before too long, a mere preview of things to come.

*You ain't seen nothin' yet.*

We pushed on to the north. Next stop, Baghdad.

Massive air strikes on the city—the vaunted "Shock and Awe"—had pre-ceded the invasion. The battle to take the city was still on, and there'd been a couple of failed attempts to kill Saddam, who had so far slipped from our grasp. The statue had not yet been pulled down, nor the museums, hospitals, office buildings, hotels, and palaces sacked, as they would be in the free-for-all follow-ing the capture of the city and the collapse of Saddam's government.

We had no idea what sort of reception to expect from the locals. How would I feel if Sacramento had been bombed by invading forces, and then they rolled their military convoys through the streets? Would I be throwing flowers?

We took a little detour off the highway and went toward the city. Soon we were passing beneath the famous "Victory Arch," a monument to Saddam built by Saddam, commemorating his triumph over Iran back in the late '80s. The grandiose arch, wide enough and high enough to drive a truck under, featured crossed swords, each held by a giant fist modelled after Saddam's actual hands. Beyond the gates, the city was a bombed-out mess, but people were going about their business amidst piles of rubble and smoldering Russian tanks. We got our-selves into a bit of a tight spot in the narrow streets, but were startled and relieved at the cheerful reception we got from the locals. Obviously, plenty of the citizens of Baghdad were more than ready for "regime change," costly though it was to them. Still, we were glad to extricate ourselves and get out of there.

On the outskirts, as we were finding our way back to the highway, I beheld an intriguing sight. An Iraqi man wearing a flowing white traditional dish-dash robe was hanging dozens of little clear plastic bags of water on the branches of a tree; inside each bag, a goldfish darted about, catching the glint of the afternoon sun. What was I seeing? A signal, a work of art, a ceremony? Or just commerce? Whatever it was, it was a grace note of bright incongruity in a bleak landscape.

We were now about to enter what was known as the Sunni Triangle, a region northwest of Baghdad densely populated by Sunni Muslims. The people in the Sunni Triangle were known for their fierce loyalty to the soon-to-be-deposed leader. Throughout most of the Arab world, the Sunni were the majority; in Iraq, it was the opposite. The Sunnis were a roughly 20 percent minority, vastly outnumbered by the Shia, but Saddam had been born Sunni, and so that minority had been a powerful one during his reign, and at the government and upper-class level, a ruling clique. Now that Saddam was about to be ripped up by the roots, the chances of something other than flowers being thrown at us in this part of the country went way up; the northerly point of the so-called triangle was the little city of Tikrit, Saddam's hometown. Now would not be the time or place for complacency.

We pushed on. Humans were not the only inhabitants of this mysterious land who watched us with interest. We were startled at the sight of giant desert lizards standing up on their hind legs next to the highway like four-foot-tall T. Rexes, gazing at us in a distinctly non-warm-and-fuzzy way as we passed by.

# CHAPTER 5

# ILL WINDS

On the afternoon of the next day, I stood at the edge of an Olympic-swimming-pool-sized pit dug by a bulldozer a few hours before, so furious that I was afraid a vein in my head might explode. In my hand, held aloft in the Lady Liberty position, an emergency flare hissed and sparked. In the pit in front of me a huge pile of sarin-soaked rubber Russian hazmat suits glistened with aviation fuel. My throat was raw from shouting.

Under orders from Col. Maloney, I was about to toss the flare into the pit. As I moved my arm back to make the throw, the crowd of officers, Maloney included, took off running in the opposite direction.

I tossed the flare, then moved away fast myself in the direction of the prevailing wind as the pit ignited with a monstrous *fwump*! A column of dense black smoke rose, and then, exactly as I'd warned Maloney it would, the smoke went just so high, stopped its ascent and spread horizontally across the sky.

We were at the airbase near the city of Balad, about fifty miles north of Baghdad. We'd arrived after dark the night before, and could see nothing of the landscape except mysterious flames burning in the distance in every direction. Later, we'd find out we were seeing massive file and document fires, the Iraqis burning everything they could as they fled.

In the morning, we gathered and stored in a dozen big trailers piles and piles of whatever papers escaped being burned. We had as yet no knowledge of what was in the files, which were all in Arabic, or why they were being destroyed. We explored the base and found a few things we were not expecting: a crematorium, complete with bone fragments, and the massive stash of old Russian poison-soaked hazmat suits. It was Maloney's bright idea to dig the big ditch, truck the hazmat suits over, dump them in, and then burn them.

You've probably heard of sarin. It's one of the more charming human inventions, brought to us by the Germans in 1938, a toxic nerve agent capable of killing a person or animal within seconds when in its vaporized (gas) form. Saddam had used it, along with other types of nerve gas, against the Kurds in the famous 1988 massacre at Halabja.

When I stood at the edge of the pit with the flare in my hand, my blood boiled and my head reverberated with the angry words Maloney and I had hurled at each other.

"You can't do this," I'd said. "Sarin is *extremely* volatile even without fire to help it along. Even without the sarin, just burning that much rubber would be a disaster! The winds today guarantee that the smoke will go everywhere, not just up!"

The more I argued, the more he dug in and the redder his face went.

"That's an *order*, Sergeant Ford!"

What I saw then was that having his authority challenged offended him way worse than the possibility of poisoning every living thing within miles. Reason had exactly nothing to do with it. And I was sure it was why he then chose me to light the fire: because I'd dared to challenge him. I was older than he was, vastly more accomplished and experienced, and he knew it. So he put me in my place, with everyone watching.

In the days, weeks, and months that followed, the pit never stopped burning as a steady flow of debris—human waste, medical waste, industrial waste, tires, plain old garbage and trash, excess jet fuel, solvents, plastics of every sort—got tossed in. The stench was beyond diabolical. The perverse contempt expressed by this made me think of twisted children performing a sick experiment. What I didn't know at the moment I tossed the flare was that this was quite possibly the first of hundreds more of these infernal "burn pits" that would smolder perpetually throughout Iraq, night and day, over the next ten years of the occupation, sending their hellish poisonous smoke into the sky.

These "eternal flames" would soon come to be recognized as beacons proclaiming the presence of coalition forces, and anyone spending any time at all near them, or especially, tending them, would develop a clinging, deep, sore, persistent cough, and later, alarmingly high rates of cancer, multiple sclerosis, heart and respiratory disease, neurological disorders, and other mysterious afflictions (an eventual likely "burn pit" casualty would be Joe Biden's son Beau, who served in Iraq and died of brain cancer in 2015).

I myself got the "burn pit" cough almost immediately, and have it to this day. The pit seemed to me to be perfectly emblematic of the general chaos of this invasion and occupation and the incompetence of my command. A conviction that I'd gone to war with not-so-funny clowns had already begun to form; the sight of those brave leaders of men scuttling away as the flare went into the pit confirmed it.

Recognizing a disaster in the making when I saw one, I told Maloney and another of my commanders, his close buddy and compatriot Capt. Hector Segura (not his real name), that I'd noted the names of everyone present that day, officers in particular.

Segura was an American citizen, but born and bred in El Salvador, a country infamous for its brutal, oppressive military and high murder rate. It got that way in part with plenty of help from the good old USA and its aggressive policy, especially under Ronald Reagan, of military support for Latin American strongmen and of interfering, bloodily, in insurrections against those strongmen by the common people. That policy was an extension of the Cold War, a grotesque inverted distortion of values where regular people rising up against dictators were characterized as "Communists" and therefore the enemy, killable and crushable. Kidnapping, torture, and "disappearing" were honed to a fine art in that part of the world. There would be, eventually, a direct and sinister Iraq connection to all of that, which we'll get to, but for now, suffice it to say that it's a cruel place; it was El Salvador where three American nuns working for social justice were raped and murdered by Salvadoran National Guard soldiers in 1980 as civil war brewed. That's the world from which Segura sprang.

He and Maloney had clearly "bonded." They were both short, maybe 5'6", and were afflicted with "short guy" attitude. They were a pair. I warned these two:

"If this turns out to be the catastrophe I think it is, I have your names. I'll make sure it's known who was responsible. I'll file."

File? Sigh. If I'd had any idea then of what lay ahead. . . .

And soon there was a shakeup: Col. Thomas Pappas, a not-overly-popular guy, came in and replaced the well-liked Col. Charles Parrish. Now, along with Maloney and Segura, there were three unpopular commanders, all much higher in rank but younger than I was, and they quickly formed a three-amigos-type union.

What sort of guy was Pappas? Well, a while after he came in, he decided he wanted a belated "changing of the guard" ceremony at Balad, and he commanded various units stationed elsewhere to attend. A Humvee, traveling seventy-five miles across open desert, carrying a unit under orders to be at this event, hurried to get through what was known to be hostile territory, the driver going too fast for the terrain.

The Humvee flipped, killing three of the soldiers aboard.

# CHAPTER 6

# HEARTS AND MINDS

**W**hat do we need to know about the problems between Sunni and Shia?" I politely asked the small group of Iraqi men with whom we sat.

"There are no problems," said the village mayor. "No issues. That is all a western fabrication."

"Ah," I said, and waited.

"We have had Sunni, Shia, and even Persians in this village for a long time, all coexisting peacefully. If problems ever arise, we will know you caused them," he said, only half-jokingly. "Saddam made it quite clear to us that he would not tolerate ethnic partitioning. He told us that we are not Sunni and Shia Iraqis, nor Kurdish Iraqis or Persian Iraqis: we are all simply Iraqis."

I thought of the brothers on their camel, but of course said nothing.

When I wasn't lighting burn pits under duress, I had real work to do. My crew and I were on a goodwill and reconnaissance visit to the tiny town of Adu Jael, just a couple of miles west of Balad. It was obvious that for most of the people there, we were the first Americans they'd ever seen. The welcome had been almost embarrassingly effusive. They cheered and clapped us on the back as if we were heroes.

Now we sat inside a mud brick house with the mayor and other town leaders. A big carved silver tumbler of ice-cold water was passed from hand to hand, everyone taking a swallow. This was no time to be germ-conscious; the mutual water-sipping was clearly quasi-ceremonial, and at the very least, a ritual of friendship. To be included was to be honored. It would have been the height of bad manners, not to mention lousy diplomacy, to turn it down. I marveled at the way the Iraqis always seemed to be able to produce cold water, no matter how hot and dry the surroundings. It felt like magic.

And the mayor told us a story: A few years before, Saddam's presidential motorcade had been passing close to Adu Jael. Shots were allegedly fired from the direction of the village. Saddam responded by coming into town, yanking 123 men and boys from the population, and executing them on the spot.

And I wondered: *What will happen to this enforced coexistence when we've removed Saddam from power and interfered with the complicated dynamics required for a minority to successfully oppress a majority?* It was a sobering thought, especially in light of the remark made just a few moments before: if problems ever arise, we will know you caused them.

I couldn't have known it at the time, but eventually, Saddam would be condemned to death for that mass execution in Adu Jael. Of the countless atrocities and crimes against humanity committed by Saddam, that would be the one that would put the rope around his neck.

On another goodwill trip to a different village soon after, my crew and I were greeted with the same warmth and open arms by the locals, and in particular by a boy of about fifteen literally leaping with joy. With what looked to me like a golden light of welcome in his eyes, the boy bounded up to me, grabbed my face, kissed me on both cheeks, threw his head back, and sent rapturous thanks to Allah skyward. Then he danced down to the next vehicle to give the same welcome. I was pretty sure that for these people, too, we were the first Americans they'd ever seen.

I was dazzled by the purity of the kid's ecstatic welcome. Later, I was disgusted by the boorishness of some of my associates. When we got back to the base, Segura approached me and asked, perfectly seriously, why I was "kissing a man" at the village.

I soon found out what happened: a couple of my people, the aforementioned May Ling and one Stavros Papadakis (not his real name), my supposed compatriots, had radioed in their version of the boy's welcome, thinking it was a big hoot. More disturbing to me than the stupid joke was their cultural ignorance and crass lack of appreciation for what they had actually witnessed. Worse, they

had no grasp at all of the moment's importance: that the goodwill of these people was ours, and that we should guard it and cultivate it, that this was our job,
the very reason we were here. On a return visit later to the same village, I was
swarmed by joyous children, who rushed out of hiding in a big welcome. May
and Stavros sat sullenly in the Humvee, pouting. *Bad manners,* I thought, *and
exactly the wrong attitude. Not helpful at all.*

These two, May and Stavros, were already on my radar. May, the sleep-
ing-tent tease, now seemed to be hooking up with Stavros, a tough little Greek
who showed signs of being a tightly-wrapped package of toxic grudges with a
twitchy temper. They made a lovely pair.

But just when I'd get into a grim or discouraged state of mind, one of those
grace notes this mysterious land produced from time to time, all the more magical because of the incongruity, would reveal itself and turn my head around
completely.

On one of our goodwill expeditions, I was out of our vehicle and in a narrow
space between walls within a village, walking backward, guiding the driver of
our Humvee, which had maybe an inch of clearance of its mirrors on either side.
I'd paused, and felt something touch my leg, ever so lightly. I looked down and
beheld a blond, blue-eyed boy of perhaps four, dressed in a little white dish-
dash, looking up at me calmly and steadily.

This was not the first time I'd seen red-haired, light-haired, and even blond
children in Iraq, but this one was almost translucent, his eyes the palest rob-
in's-egg blue I'd seen anywhere, his hair flaxen.

I suppose it was the combination of his ethereal coloring and his utter trust
and fearlessness, but I was just about knocked over with enchantment. I picked
him up and held him while he explored my helmet, gear, and face with delicate
fingers. Meanwhile, his mother had appeared, and waited nearby with a nervous smile. I smiled back as reassuringly as I could, handed the boy to her, and
she hurried away. I can still feel the touch of those little fingers, so light but so
definite.

Do transcendent moments come in clusters? I'd heard that one of the major
bird migration stopovers in the Middle East was near the air base, and soon

after the encounter with the little angel boy, I went on an excursion by myself after noticing cottonwood trees in the distance, a sure sign of water, surprisingly abundant here and there in Iraq, thanks to the two mighty rivers.

What I found was an exquisite hundred-acre pond, a true oasis. I stepped into another world, of lush beauty—huge, ancient twisted willows, giant cottonwoods, palms, and eucalyptus, and staggeringly abundant bird life: ducks, geese, swans, long-legged storks, herons, and egrets. Today, I was looking through my binoculars at something other than dust plumes on the horizon or military vehicles in the distance. The peace and tranquility amidst the calls, cries, whistles, squawks, and splashing of birds going about their ancient business transported me. Here was the other end of the sensory spectrum from the burn pit, the Highway of Death, the weapons factories.

I started walking, exploring the banks of the pond. And then I stopped, stared, blinked, and seriously asked myself if maybe I was in a technicolor dream.

Before me, next to the water, was a Russian radio truck, the top part of it intact and recognizable but the rest of it melted into a layered puddle at least thirty feet in diameter, smooth and shiny as glass. I stepped onto that hard, smooth, glassy metal surface—unwisely, in retrospect, but I couldn't resist. The combination of the wild natural beauty of the setting and the melted truck were beyond surreal, like something Salvador Dali might have conjured.

What could have done this? I had no idea.

A few days later, on another excursion, my crew and I found a mint-condition, fully-equipped Russian MIG29 fighter jet camouflaged near a wall in a vineyard within a small village. We reported the find to our command.

When we returned a couple of days later, we found it right where we'd left it, but melted, just like the radio truck, and with laser-like precision; there was zero damage to the nearby wall or anything else in its vicinity. Now the mystery was doubled, tripled: *What sort of devilish weapon could do this?* I had no clue, and neither did anybody else. I knew of the existence of long-distance particle beams, a legacy of the "star wars" defense system, able to shatter stone and metal, but *melt* them? This was something altogether different. And in whose hands was this weapon? Was it mere coincidence that we reported the existence of this plane just a few days ago, and now it was a Dali-esque puddle? That seemed unlikely.

Most of all—and this was the one that haunted me—how strange was it that I should have stumbled across the melted radio truck at the pond just a few days before we found the soon-to-be-melted plane in the village? I hadn't mentioned the melted truck to anyone.

Everything I do in my various lines of work is predicated on the real, the empirical, the solid three-dimensional facts. I didn't deal in the slippery and insubstantial. This business, though, was just plain spooky.

Not quite so spooky but just as surreal was a discovery we made near the base. Acting on a tip, we found, as if we were walking onto a movie set, a perfect little Potemkin Village of gaily-painted Russian-style cottages, complete with fully functional bathtubs, a rarity in Iraq. The village had, we surmised, been set up to make the Russian technicians assisting the Iraqis feel at home.

We called in a report, and within thirty minutes the combat engineers showed up with a HET (Heavy Equipment Transport), a monster vehicle straight out of Mad Max: three sets of driving wheels with man-high tires, designed to go over any terrain, this one pulling a huge heavy-duty bed with a combat version of a D-9 Caterpillar 'dozer, surely one of the more Godzilla-like machines ever invented.

With a roar, the D-9 fired up, rolled off the HET, lowered its blade, and in about four passes, the Russian village was rubble. It had been less than an hour from the time we radioed in our report. And I thought to myself: *A good measure of the embarrassment and danger to a bureaucracy's credibility is how fast they "take care" of something.*

When I called it a Potemkin Village, I wasn't just being picturesque. Though the cottages had been real and functional, they hid an elaborate secret. Underneath, we found a huge, major, clandestine oil-pumping station. I pictured it: Russian technicians, tending to the pumping station, with direct, discreet access from within the fake Russian village. More strangeness in a strange land . . .

Soon after the day of the Russian village, the company chaplain invited me to come along on another goodwill expedition. I was navigating, a map in my hands, but was soon baffled by the actual roads we encountered—rough, rutted, unpaved farm roads, mainly—which didn't match up at all with the map. Pretty soon we were lost. On a hunch, I told the driver to take a turn onto another road, but that road gradually narrowed to the point where we had barely two inches of solid ground on either side of our convoy of four Humvees.

The pleasant jaunt was now a tense, hairy situation. The road could peter out to nothing, stranding us, putting us in the sitting-duck situation, ripe for ambush, that was always on our minds. We crept forward, though, and unclenched as the road gradually widened.

We were grinding along at no more than five miles per hour, and I was letting out a big breath of relief, when I looked out the window and saw what I knew right away was not a desert dog: a wolf. Big, rangy and lean, he moved out of the way of the intruders, not in any sort of hurry, but watching us with cool interest. Then he paused, perhaps twenty feet away, made direct eye contact with me, and held it.

It was a fraught moment. *I know you*, the wolf seemed to be saying.

It was the Cherokee in me that looked back into those perfectly sentient yellow wolf eyes and thought: *This is an omen. Of what, I don't know. But an omen.*

In the next moment, the wolf broke the eye contact and loped away. It was then I remembered a long-ago National Geographic article mentioning the place with the highest rate of wolf attacks on humans in the world: Iraq. Despite the heat, a tiny chill caressed my forehead.

We pushed on. We were on a levee, approaching the village, when we found ourselves unable to go any further because our way was blocked, and not by a broken-down pickup truck or a pile of debris, but by a gleaming, mint condition, fully-equipped Russian MIG29 fighter jet, exactly like the one we'd found in the other village. This MIG was in even better condition, if possible, than that first one before it was melted. Ever wary of booby traps, I climbed up and entered the cockpit with infinite care. The crew attached a cable to the plane, and with me manipulating the rudder pedals and other controls, we were able to tow it onto an adjoining levee so our convoy could proceed.

Back at the base later on that same day, my Humvee was parked at the perimeter while I sat in the front passenger seat doing paperwork. A group of six or seven Iraqi men approached. They were civilians, unarmed, but noticeably less welcoming than the villagers we'd so far encountered.

The man who seemed to be the leader of the group addressed me in a forthright way, speaking through my translator.

"Are you going to leave us the way you did last time? My sons taken and slaughtered? Our lives ruined? Are you going to annihilate us?"

I did my best to reassure him. "I hope not. That isn't our intent."

We were still speaking when I heard a gasp from May, in the Humvee with me.

"Greg," she said, "My God! You've got to help her!"

I looked up and recoiled: emerging from the group of men, a girl, perhaps seven years old, drenched in dried blood, walked toward me holding her arms out in front of her, plainly in shock. Skin hung in shreds off her limbs, torso, and face, the lids peeled back from her eyes. She was covered in flies.

The man who'd been speaking through the translator told me this was his daughter, that she and some other kids had found what they thought was a toy. It detonated just as the girl picked it up. And I knew: A cluster bomblet! In the case of the type she found, the resemblance to a toy is what makes it so lethal, and that resemblance is intentional. Cluster bombs are the devil's piñata; a big canister, packed with small bombs, is dropped. It shatters, scattering the bomblets packed inside. Some explode on impact, some do not. The ones that don't explode because they have a timer inside them preventing them from going off right away roll, bounce, and come to a stop. Round, pretty, innocent-looking and about the size of an orange, they too often attract the attention of children. Inside is a tumbler switch, activated when an inquisitive hand picks it up. Some private arms manufacturer surely held the patent on this fiendish device, and made huge profits from it.

I got my medical kit, spoke to her as soothingly as I could, striving to hide my own shock, and gingerly applied Betadine to her wounds where I could.

This small, slight child was as stoic as any man or soldier I'd ever seen and made not a sound or a whimper while I worked on her.

Deeply shaken, I filled out a medical order form, signed it, and had the translator tell the father to take the child to the field hospital at the base. I didn't have a lot of confidence that he would do this; she was, after all, only a girl.

# CHAPTER 7

# THE SHELTERING SKY

As we raced down the road south out of Balad, I saw two Apache helicopters above the horizon in the distance, coursing along, apparently aimlessly, as if they were just looking around. Then I noticed the Apaches "putting on the brakes," so to speak, rearing back, hesitating for a few moments before lowering their noses and both of them shooting an arc light toward the ground. The 'copters went into a hover, then started backing up as if they were in trouble. We halted where we were and gaped as an orange-lit mushroom cloud bloomed thousands of feet up into the sky. The force of the explosion traveled along miles of ground in an instant, reaching the Humvees we were in, lifting them a couple of feet, propelling them backward a yard or so and slamming them back to earth, shaking us up like forks in a drawer.

By now, I'd learned to expect the unexpected. But the term can always take on new meaning by an order of magnitude.

My unit and I had got a tip one day that "Chemical Ali"—Saddam's first cousin and a wanted war criminal who earned his nickname for his role in the infamous gassing of the Kurds in the late 1980s—had been seen at a certain petrol station to the south, and that this might be a chance to nab him.

We jumped into our vehicles and took off. We'd only gone a few miles when we spotted the Apaches. Now we sat dumbstruck in our Humvees that had just levitated and landed, our teeth nearly rattled out of our heads.

The spectacle was far enough away from our vantage that it was eerily silent. We watched as the heat of the monstrous eruption sucked up hundreds of massive thousand-pound air-deployable bombs. The bombs rose to the top of the mushroom formation like feathers in a pillow fight, emerged spinning and throwing brilliant sparks, then detonated as they were forcefully hurled in all directions. Two giant black smoke rings a mile high and at least a mile wide encircled the entire light show like some heavenly nimbus. The entire formation started to march north, toward where we were watching. All of this took place in about the space of a minute. I saw a spotter plane appear, no doubt to find out what the hell was going on, and fly through the smoke rings as if in an otherworldly air show.

Only later did I learn what happened, though not why it happened. The Apache helicopters had fired missiles down into a major weapons facility southwest of Balad. The missiles had pierced one of hundreds of underground bunkers, setting off what looked for a few moments like the apocalypse itself. If Chemical Ali had been at that petrol station, he was gone by the time we got there.

Colorful eruptions can occur in many forms. Present in Iraq at that time were scattered units of famously tough expat Iranian fighters called the Mujahedeen Khalq, a.k.a. MEK. They had a complicated, controversial history—they'd started out as left-leaning idealists dedicated to overthrowing the Shah, but after the Ayatollah Khomeini came to power, the relatively progressive MEK clashed with the new grimly theocratic government and MEK had been exiled and labelled a "terrorist" group by the regime.

During Saddam's eight-year war with Iran, MEK had fought on the side of Saddam and the Iraqis against Iran. By the 2003 invasion and the ousting of Saddam, MEK had made it clear that they now wished to side with the coalition forces. I had seen them near Balad, and was astonished when the hatch on one of their personnel carriers flipped open and armed female Iranian fighters in full black hijabs with brilliant red scarves and flashing eyes poured out. I was seriously impressed by the toughness and dedication of both the male and female Iranian MEK fighters.

In the complicated and ever-shifting factional crossfire, it was not always clear who was the enemy and who was not. Some Americans had decided that the MEK, having once sided with Saddam, were "terrorists" and our enemies. A couple of the fighters were brought, wounded, to the field hospital in Balad, and it was not certain who tried to kill them—Iraqis or Americans. I went to the field hospital to investigate, to see these wounded fighters, because it was suspected they were actually shot by Americans.

While I was there, I established rapport with some of the MEK fighters, and was able to recruit them as assets, thanks to a nurse who was there that day and who made introductions. Imagine the invaluable intelligence resource these guys represented—Iranian fighters who had once allied themselves to Saddam but who now sided with us. Think of who and what they knew. Did I get acknowledgment of any sort from my command for such a recruiting coup? You can probably guess the answer.

I met with the American surgeon who was treating them, and my own examination of the wounded men made me think that indeed they had been shot by Americans, who failed to recognize that these were "friends," and not by Iraqis. The surgeon agreed: the combination of high-velocity bullets and the fact that many of the wounds were neck shots pointed to American perps. While I was discussing this with the surgeon, an arrogant, self-satisfied sort of chap, he happened to mention that some doofus medic had had the gall to write up an order for him to treat a little girl wounded in an explosion. What a waste of resources, the guy seemed to be implying.

"And whatever stupid idiot wrote up that order gave the girl's father directions so he could find us. Now he'll be bothering us all the time."

"Yes," I said. "And that stupid idiot is standing in front of you right now. I'm the one who wrote that order."

The surgeon sputtered for a moment, then hastened to add that the girl had been treated and survived. It was a profoundly satisfying moment for me, the last such moment I'd have for a long, long time.

# CHAPTER 8

# WHAT LIES BENEATH

The child, perhaps three or four years old, with her gleaming dark hair and eyes and wearing a red velvet dress, was a glowing little jewel in the industrial drabness around us. Holding her hand was her father, who put me in mind of a tough hombre out of a spaghetti western, big black moustache and all. He spoke excellent English and was, I'd just learned, a colonel in the Iraqi army, a pilot, though today he was in civilian clothing. He had approached me while I was out doing guard duty at a water treatment plant on the Tigris River near the airbase. We hit it off right away.

While we were talking, a US military helicopter approached, flying low up the river, no more than six or seven feet above the water.

"Watch this," the colonel said. And he asked his little daughter, in English: "What is that coming toward us?" The child answered immediately, saying something that sounded like "hibache," her baby Iraqi mouth's pronunciation of "Apache." I was struck by the child's precocity and knowledge. I could also see that to her innocent eyes, those flying death machines were wondrous, magical.

I, though, was uneasy. Fresh from the Ripley's Believe It Or Not weapons bunker celestial conflagration, I knew how well-equipped those Apaches were, and how trigger-happy the yahoos in them could be. The Apache approaching us now might just take a notion to mow us down where we stood and ask questions later. The Apache seemed to hesitate; it was like the moment in a sci-fi movie when you know the aliens have seen you. I'd successfully hidden my apprehension from the colonel and the child, but I felt my own breathing and heart rate returning to normal when the helicopter moved past us and flew on up the river.

The colonel and I liked the cut of each other's jib. After we'd talked a while, he gave me a long appraising look and then seemed to make a decision.

And he said:

"You know, do you not, that you invaded our country illegally? We will go together to al qaeda tomorrow. I have something important to show you."

Say *what?* We'll go to *Al Qaeda?* I must have reared back a little.

"My apologies," he said, and laughed. "That's simply Arabic for 'the base.' I mean, of course, the air base. We will go to the air base tomorrow."

I knew, of course, that the term had an innocent Arabic meaning, but in that context, it had come across just a little differently. We both laughed then.

He paused with dramatic significance before his next words. "We knew you were coming. George W. Bush announced it to the world in his speech a few days before you arrived. This was when we moved weapons, had the farmers pull the Russian jet fighters out of hiding and such."

The MIG on the levee! So that's how it got there!

The colonel knew that I and my unit were intel people and made it clear that he had purposely sought me out. Evidently our goodwill visits to neighboring villages had not gone unnoticed.

He gave me information then, of the sort an intel agent dreams of, about the uses and deployment of weapons, the outside help the Iraqis had got from the Russians, Yugoslavians, and East Germans—the latter specializing in bunker-building—how the Russian fighter-bombers had been modified in order to accommodate American weapons, and much, much more, all of it indicative of a vast web of clandestine alliances, deals, and pacts.

The ground we stood on while we talked was so hot I felt my toenails burning inside my boots, but I could hardly break away from this fascinating, pricelessly valuable conversation. I noticed that the colonel wore rubber-tire-soled sandals, sensible footwear for this environment.

We rendezvoused the next morning. The colonel escorted me to one of hundreds of nondescript buildings on the base we'd taken over. This one, less than two hundred yards from Col. Maloney's field office, looked like any other.

We went in, and I found myself looking at a set of metal stairs descending into a black hole. A blast of heat rose from the depths. And I thought: *This must be what it's like to descend into hell.* And I wondered: *Am I being set up? Have I seen the sun for the last time? Am I going down the rabbit hole?*

My Cherokee blood stirred. *If there are spirits down there, they aren't good ones.*

My training in espionage kicked in, and I watched the colonel intently for sweatiness, twitchiness, and unusual motions of eyes or facial muscles, involuntary giveaways when a person is being duplicitous. And I had to maintain a calm, unsuspicious demeanor while I was doing it. I was trained in that, too. To be an agent is to be, in certain situations, a tightly-contained bundle of contradictions, as well as an Oscar-worthy actor.

But the colonel led the way down the stairs, making easy conversation as he went. He asked me where I was from, and when I said California, his manner lit up in a way that would be hard to fake.

"I want to go to California someday," he said, and I relaxed a notch or two. *Unlikely he'd be talking California Dreaming if he means to blow us both to smithereens,* I thought.

My web gear was equipped with a multi-lensed light. For this descent, I switched on the red beam, less likely to trip an electronic booby-trap. My boots clanging on the metal stairs, the colonel and I went down about a story, came to a platform, and descended another story. The further down we went, the more oppressive the heat. I was in full-body armor, helmet on my head. Soon I was soaked in sweat. It was still only March, but it was hotter down here than midsummer in the desert above.

We arrived at a metal door. The colonel opened it, and we stepped inside. He switched on a dim overhead light. Revealed was a vast room, stretching into the distance. I saw big oblong open-frame crates, three times the length of a tall man, stacked in layers of two, arranged in orderly rows. Between the red glow of my lamp, the heat, and the mysterious crates, I was stunned.

"What am I looking at?" I asked.

"Please," said the Colonel, inviting me to examine a label affixed to one of the crates.

I wiped the rivulets of sweat from my face with the *keffiyah* I carried. I blinked my stinging eyes and peered at the paper. It was a bill of lading from the Carlyle Group, a giant American arms-dealing (among other enterprises) corporation, founded and run by US mega-politicians and mega-financiers, including George H. W. Bush. Here it was: a piece of the vast borderless hidden machine of interlocked war, profit, death, and commerce I'd heard about, that rules the world, run by overlords operating from the shadows.

Within the crates were P-400 bomb canisters, reconfigured at Ft. Rucker, Alabama, sold by President Bush Sr. and his Secretary of Defense Dick Cheney directly to Saddam in the days after the end of the Iran/Iraq war and before Gulf War 1, back when he was America's "friend" and CIA employee. Other bills of lading showed that some of the canisters were bought much more recently, just a couple of months before the '03 invasion.

The payload these reconfigured bombs carried were the components of VX gas, a nerve toxin so powerful that a single tiny drop on a person's skin is fatal. The weapons before us were equipped with a trigger mechanism that would cause the VX components to combine and release as the canisters floated down from the heavens, each with its own parachute. The Colonel showed me how every individual gas bomb was in a state of readiness, equipped with its own instrument panel controllable from the aircraft dropping it.

"There was a great search, was there not, for Saddam's weapons of mass destruction?" the Colonel said. "Here they are." Looking at the huge room and what it contained and knowing the deadliness of even a miniscule amount of the substance within the canisters, it occurred to me that I was in the presence of enough killing potential to end most life on earth. Weapons of mass destruction, indeed. In the public mind, the term was always associated with nuclear weapons. Here, before me, the concept instantly and chillingly redefined itself.

"So," said the Colonel. "This is what you Americans were looking for, is it not? Will you pack up your shit and leave our country now?"

Excitement coursed through me. *We can go home,* I thought. *The war is over!*

With the colonel's encouragement, and using the handy little crescent wrench on my Swiss Army knife, I reached through the open wooden slats of one of the crates, and by the red light of my lamp, removed what's called the "dispersal door" from one of the canisters. It was about the size of a Frisbee, and on it was stamped crucial information in the form of a GSN (General Service supply Number). Contained in that indelible GSN was everything about the lethal canister it was attached to: where it was made, by whom, and its exact tortuous route from Alabama to Iraq. My training kicked in, and I quickly and automatically memorized the number. Here was tangible proof of the existence of these WMD, and proof that they were apple-pie American.

The colonel knew everything about them, not just where they came from, but how they worked. He had, in his career, flown fighter bombers for Saddam and dropped similar payloads of death. He had, for instance, been part of Saddam's Halabja attack in 1988. The official verdict had been that the thousands of Kurds who died had succumbed to mustard gas, but "other nerve agents" were cited as well. According to the colonel, those "other" nerve agents included VX, dispensed in canisters identical to these.

There was a deadly choreography of stages that the various components of the gas, individually inert and harmless, went through in order to be transformed, via the miracle of chemistry, into VX, all, as I mentioned, controllable from the cockpit. The delivery system included an altitude sensor that caused the parachute to open when the mixture was ready to do its job. Pressure would build, the dispersal door would pop open, the parachute would deploy, and the canister, spewing death, would descend slowly, gently, to earth, saturating the atmosphere from high above for maximum distribution.

The colonel told me another fascinating tidbit—the fighter-bombers were permitted only enough fuel to fly from their bases to their targets, at which point, after dropping the canisters, they'd have to refuel, taking on just enough to get them back to their bases. Why? Because Saddam did not want possibly mutinous pilots taking off into the friendly skies, absconding to some other country with aircraft and weaponry.

What did it mean that these canisters had been "reconfigured" at Ft. Rucker, Alabama? It meant not merely that these were of American provenance, but that they'd been precisely adapted to be used with the particular aircraft flown by Saddam's fighters. Good old American know-how at its best. The familiar joke about the receipts for WMD turned out to be quite literally true. Here I was, looking right at such a receipt, the Carlyle bill of lading on every crate. And now I had the dispersal door in my hand. Meanwhile, the Colonel was counting the canisters. He looked at me with an expression of mild concern.

"There are twenty-eight," he said. "There should be twenty-nine. One is missing."

# CHAPTER 9

# ROGUES AND SCOUNDRELS

I saw the whirring of canny calculation behind Maloney's eyes as he listened to my story with a poker face: *How might this affect me and my career, and what might it be worth in dollars and cents?* In front of him, on his desk, was the dispersal door, where I'd just plunked it. I'd gone straight to his office, not two hundred feet from the bunker, to notify him of the stash of VX gas.

"It's real," I said. "That GSN on there doesn't lie." But his reaction to tangible proof of WMD directly under his nose was to say nothing at all to me. Instead, he stood, mumbled something about "talking" to somebody about it, and hurried from his office.

I fully expected him to go to CNN (who were on-scene and set up less than one hundred yards away), who would then swarm all over us and broadcast to the world that the WMD had been found and that the coalition would be pulling out. Yes, I actually thought that. I look back on my naiveté now and scratch my head in bewilderment. Was that really me?

The day after my descent into the bunker, still waiting to see what Maloney would do with what I told him, I was riding around the base with some other personnel, on a "docintel" mission, gathering up the plentiful remaining piles of un-burnt Iraqi documents stashed all over the air base, loading whatever we found into a trailer to be sorted through later. We came to a nondescript mud brick building, like countless others all over Iraq, but something caught my eye: an open window that just seemed to beckon. I had the driver stop. Something compelled me to approach the building.

Avoiding the door, I got my gun ready, peered through the open window, and saw an ominous shape: a single uncrated P-400 canister, exactly like the ones I saw in the bunker just the day before. Here was the missing twenty-ninth WMD, noted by the Colonel. Lying cross-wise atop it was a Sparrow air-to-air missile.

Peering into the building, I saw that the control panel on the side of the small missile was open, and there was an electrical cord leading from it down onto the floor, then snaking under a straw mat just inside the door, ready for an unwary foot upon the pressure plate that was surely beneath the mat. An instruction manual, in English, lay open atop the canister, left there by whoever wired the pressure plate and then left the building. A booby trap: crude, obvious, but doubtless effective. *Jesus,* I thought, *who set this up, and why? Who was it meant for?*

My heart pounded as I contemplated the pent-up destructive power just a few feet from me. I thanked my own good judgment—and training—that I did not step through the door. Reluctant to even disturb the air around me, I withdrew my face from the window.

I had a complicated flood of reactions to what I just saw: *Are we or are we not "liberators?"* The crudeness of the booby-trap, in such contrast to the mega-high-tech killing apparatus it was meant to trigger, spoke to me of an intertangled web of conflicts stretching back in time and into the future, the true players unknown even to each other, the supposed reasons for war advertised to the public nothing but a mirage. The rig in the hut seemed perfectly symbolic. *Have we, the American military, stumbled into a booby-trap on a giant scale?*

Thinking about it much later, I developed a theory: that I was getting a preview of what would come to be called the "counterinsurgency."

At the time, I noted the position of the hut relative to both the prevailing wind and the direction from which the Americans approached the airbase; had the trap been tripped, the wind would have carried the VX directly toward the invaders. Biological weapons sensors would have been set off, and all forward motion would have stopped.

As for the stash revealed to me by the Iraqi colonel, a British team of experts specializing in the neutralization and disposal of bombs was brought in immediately, and the deadly stockpile was removed. A new "burn pit" was dug, a high-tech arc furnace installed in the pit, and the canisters, along with the bills of lading from Carlyle, were destroyed in its 5000-degree heat while an officer named Pete Fischer (not his real name), who carried a video camera with him everywhere, recorded the event. A couple of years later, Fischer would mention this footage and the discovery of the WMD during an interview on *Nightline* with Ted Koppel, only to have the plug pulled on him the instant the topic came up.

The booby-trapped twenty-ninth canister was similarly destroyed when I led an American bomb squad to the mud brick building, but the Carlyle bill of lading on that one found its way into my pocket.

———————

Was it paranoia, or was I sensing actual personality changes in everyone in my vicinity? In the days following my report of the monster stash of WMD, there were sideways looks, slippery glances, darting eyes, and tension in the air. My unit was due to head north to Samarra. At first, the word from my commanders was that I wouldn't be going.

"Right," I said. "Of course. You probably want me around to explain all about the WMD."

Now I was dead sure: I was not just being paranoid. Their furtive faces when I spoke those words made it obvious something was up.

So I probed a little further: "I'll just head on over to CNN and give them an interview, since I'm the guy who found the stash. And I'm sure the weapons inspectors will want to hear all about it, too."

Now I saw looks of sheer panic, and within twenty minutes, I had my orders: Get your gear together. You're going to Samarra. And that was the end of it; no more was heard about the WMD. No CNN, no announcement to the world. It quickly became apparent that my elation was for nothing; the war was not over, the Americans and the rest of the coalition forces would not be "packing up" and going home anytime soon.

Why would the discovery of WMD, one of the major "justifications" for this invasion, be buried, suppressed, and not trumpeted to the world? Wouldn't such a discovery be vindication and triumph for Bush and Cheney? As in: See? We told you! Saddam *did* have WMD! Just like we said!

Mysterious on the face of it, yes, but given the facts—that WMD *were* found and the discovery *was* buried—we must try to put ourselves in their heads in order to penetrate their elaborate scheming. Here's what I think: They never had any intention of actually "finding" WMD—at least, not *publicly*. They knew the effect on the popular mind of the frightening term "Weapons of Mass Destruction," and knew, in the wake of 9/11 and the new scary world we now inhabited, that it was the best possible hypnotic mantra, repeated over and over, to get us to buy into an invasion of Iraq.

They knew quite well that there was a possibility of a major stash of WMD in Iraq, because they knew they'd been sold to Saddam by Bush Sr. and Rumsfeld, and had been manufactured by Carlyle, a company partly owned by Bush Sr. and on whose board George W. Bush sat, inconvenient facts that could not be allowed to emerge into the light of day. Sure, they wanted to find those WMD, if Saddam had not moved them or destroyed them, but they wanted to find them *in secret* in order to swiftly destroy the stash themselves, and most important, destroy the evidence tracing them back to the Carlyle Group, Poppy Bush, and Dubya. They weren't going to let silly details monkey wrench their grand scheme. Risky though it was to cry "WMD!" in the run-up to war, they must have found the power of those syllables irresistibly useful in selling their illegal, pre-planned aggression, even though to do so risked bringing attention to their own nefarious double-dealing. I think they enjoyed the game.

Remember, we went in even though no weapons had been found, the excuse being that though Saddam might not have those weapons now, he surely once did, but got rid of them, or else had hidden them so well that we just hadn't found them yet and so we had to invade in order to keep looking for them. Either way, he was guilty, and needed to be punished and deposed.

Once the weapons were actually found at Balad, and clandestinely destroyed with no announcement to the world, the pretext of a "search" could continue.

Which meant the successful and highly profitable invasion, occupation, and "regime change," all centering around profit, oil, and regional control and which had been in the works for many years pre-9/11, the *real* reasons we invaded, could roll on without interference. They had promises to keep to their "stockholders," you might say.

Complicated and confusing, yes, but only because it's almost impossible for most of us to grasp the level of greed, cynicism, and the quantities of money involved and the complexity of the layers of interlocking lies greasing the whole diabolical mechanism.

As for Maloney, I'd figure out in time that he chose to not report it to the world, as he should have, but instead contacted the Pentagon, because he had an idea that the top brass there would want the discovery suppressed, and that there would be possible rewards and promotions for him if he facilitated the cover-up. And he was right.

Why, you ask, didn't I go to CNN on my own and tell them what I'd seen? Remember, I was a trained intelligence agent. We were at war. However strong my urge to hop over to where the reporters and the cameras would hungrily grab up my story and broadcast it to every television in the world, my training was stronger. The first rule of intelligence is discretion, restraint, and keeping a cool head. So I stayed cool and held back. I'd change my mind later, of course, after what would prove to be a steep learning curve. But I was still in restraint mode on that day.

It was only March 29; I could scarcely believe I'd been in Iraq for less than a week.

*Samarra:* The very name resonated with history and legend. I was glad to leave Balad, the duplicity and the stinking burn pit behind.

# CHAPTER 10

# CITY OF GOLD

I know where your woman soldier is," sneered the detainee. He was an impressive-looking fellow, almost a cartoon version of a "terrorist," with a countenance that looked as if it had been assembled from bits and pieces of westerners' most fearful stereotypical imaginings: swarthy, black-eyed, beetle-browed, radiating defiance and a pure, focused kind of zeal, heavy black beard growing high up on his cheeks.

He was talking about the missing Jessica Lynch. And he added with a leer: "We are showing her a real good time."

This guy was one of three suspected Mukhabarat (Saddam's notoriously ruthless state intelligence agency) operatives brought in on the first night in our new quarters in Samarra. You may have heard of him: his name was Abu Bakr al-Baghdadi, future leader of ISIS, though neither he nor I could have known it at the time. The night I questioned him, he was known as al Agazzi al-Baghdadi. He was apparently unable to resist spilling what he knew about Lynch, no doubt relishing what he thought would be our reaction.

I was practiced in the art of when and how to show anger, helped in this case by authenticity. I leaned in and lasered a murderous look at the smug sonofabitch's face.

"You," I said, "are under US custody and control right now, and will be until she is found." And I added: "Do you see these two Shia policemen there?" I indicated the pair of guys who looked as if they'd been supplied by central casting: big, armed, fearless, ready and eager for the settling of ancient scores. "If we learn that she's been abused, they're going to make a point of doing everything to you that's been done to her." I paused for emphasis. "Everything."

Swarthy though he was, Baghdadi's face paled by several shades, and I could hardly write fast enough to keep up as he babbled info about her location. As it would turn out, and Baghdadi seemed to not know it (and neither did we) on the night we had him in custody, Lynch had already been released by her captors and taken to the hospital in Nasiriya. She would be rescued within days, on April 1, with a lot of help from kindly Iraqi civilians and medical people and despite some American blunders.

Was Baghdadi speaking the truth about the "showing her a real good time" part? Judging by his reaction when I threatened to have the Shia policeman reciprocate in kind, it's likely. If she was raped, it was while she was still in the hands of the Iraqi military who first captured her, and not in the hospital where she was taken. What was plain was that he got big pleasure out of taunting us with the image of a captured female American soldier at the mercy of rampaging Iraqi soldiers.

———————

We'd arrived in Samarra that same day. It's a short ride from Balad to Samarra, but a world away. I'd gazed in wonder at the dome of the Golden Mosque materializing in the distance, glinting and ethereal, as we approached the fabled city. It was easy to imagine how it was for travelers in other times, arriving by horse or camel, catching their first glimpse. Samarra had been the gold-trading center of the Middle East for centuries. We arrived to a city taken over by the Americans only hours before with scarcely a shot fired.

Samarra lived up to its storied reputation—in addition to the Golden Mosque (as yet intact; in 2006, its ancient golden dome would be blown up), architectural marvels such as the Spiral Mosque (which I climbed), the Garden of Allah and the Blue Minaret abounded, along with majestic ancient ruins. The archaeologist in me yearned to just wander through this city of wonders.

Samarra had also been the headquarters of Saddam's Baathist Party, part of the powerful Sunni minority. I and my fellow intel agents set ourselves up in the main police station in Samarra, and soon saw a dark side to the splendor.

Exploring the police station, we discovered a little room in the back. The vibes were distinctly bad; there were chains on the walls and hooks dangling from the ceiling, a legacy of Saddam. The police station was on a street bordering a vast old cemetery. You cannot imagine the immensity and crowdedness of this city of the dead. The proximity seemed sinister and appropriate.

But the panoramic view from the roof of the two-story police station, a tall building for Samarra, was excellent for our purposes. We could see most of the vast cemetery from up there, the roads and houses around and near it, and with the use of binoculars during the day and at night a thermal-image viewer, we could monitor all kinds of activity. With the thermal-image device, we could see the heat outlines of people moving around on the streets and around and inside the houses. We could watch for gatherings of people, monitor their motions, get familiar with patterns of behavior and deviations from those patterns. Much activity went on in the cemetery, and at night we watched the spectral images of human heat signatures moving around among the tombs and monuments like spirits of the departed.

Though I was experiencing some serious early discouragement after my commanders' reaction to the WMD discovery in Balad, I hung in there. Baghdadi was a big fish indeed. I hoped to get access, perhaps via Baghdadi, to the vast Mukhabarat data base and its thirty-five years' worth of intricate knowledge of everyone and everything going on everywhere in the Middle East, Russia, Israel, and the NATO countries.

As it happened, we were able to hold Baghdadi only for only a couple of nights. But he spent those nights in lockup with other detainees. Doubtless that interval was a highly productive meet 'n' greet for him; he would soon begin a rise to prominence and influence in ways we could not have imagined.

———————

Soon the word was out that the police station in Samarra was the place to go if you wanted to talk to the Americans. We were open for business, you might say. I made my office as comfortable and inviting as I could. I'd open a window so that a breeze might offer relief from the heat. I had tea and ice water in readiness, comfortable chairs. When I spoke to people, I made my notes by hand on a yellow legal pad. This small touch, writing by hand instead of on a computer keyboard, put people at ease, I believed, and inspired trust.

In the first couple of days there were hundreds of walk-ins, most of them ordinary citizens, some with stories to tell of abuse, torture, and punishment under Saddam, and some who were just curious. Our days were long, from pre-dawn to the wee hours. We felt compelled to hear every person who came in, because we never knew who might be bearing a trove of vital information.

For instance, I met an Egyptian lawyer who had worked for the Halliburton Corporation doing legal translation, who told me that during Gulf War 1, a US torture program was initiated at the King Khalid Air Force Base in Saudi Arabia; that Iraqis had been systematically tortured there during the run-up to Desert Storm; that certain specific "techniques" were "perfected" there, involving not just beating and physical force but the applied use of sexual humiliation and shame specific to Arab culture.

The lawyer made a startling, though believable, allegation: that Halliburton, in conjunction with the Rand Corporation, had a master plan to instigate this sort of sex-and-humiliation-type torture at various "black op" sites, to record such torture in photos and videos, and to hold those images under lock and key as "ammunition" until such time as they might be needed to divert attention away from the Persian Gulf and the Big Oil free-for-all going on there. This free-for-all would come to be known as the Halliburton Shell Game: tankers full of sweet Iraqi oil would load up at Kuwait City, sail to various US oil ports, do a GPS fix to prove that they'd arrived, get paid for the oil, and then, without actually offloading a single drop, sail back to the Persian Gulf, where the same oil would be offloaded at Kuwait City, turned into fuel for the war front, then sold by Halliburton to the US military for monstrous profits.

Basically, the American taxpayer would be underwriting the billions of dollars in spoils for these huge private corporations. Naturally, those in charge didn't want anyone taking a close look, and so the stash of naughty torture images would be in hand, ready to be released and turn all eyes in the other direction. Prurience trumps all, they calculated. This information would prove highly significant less than a year later when the Abu Ghraib crimes would sear themselves onto the collective mind of the world.

Another early walk-in was a youngish Western man dressed in Indiana Jones-style dusty khaki clothing, a *keffiyah* around his neck, an old Fedora on his head and sandals on his feet. He was deeply tanned and carried a beat-up backpack. When he opened his mouth and spoke, I was startled to hear a plain American voice. I'd expected British, or maybe Scandinavian.

He was, he told me, a freelance gem-hunter. He'd just come from a couple of years in Afghanistan, where some of the richest lodes of precious gems in the world—including emeralds, rubies, and sapphires—lie in the earth. Successful gem hunters are expert geologists; he'd come to Iraq to contract with petroleum engineers, hiring himself out to help them locate oil deposits.

"Osama bin Laden is in Afghanistan right now," he told me. "He's between Kunduz, way up in the north near Tajikistan, and another town called Hundun. The terrain between the two places is about the bleakest, barest, most barren moonscape you ever saw. He's surrounded by an entourage of maybe two hundred people. All you'd have to do to pinpoint his location and grab him would be to study the concentration of resources being used in that desolate stretch. Two hundred people in the middle of nowhere make a measurable, tangible footprint. Everyone in that part of Afghanistan knows he's there. He's yours for the bagging." He laughed and shook his head. "You Americans are so stupid."

I filed a report with my command: Possible location of bin Laden in Afghanistan. The response? Radio silence.

———

One afternoon in the first days after our arrival, a chauffeured black Mercedes limousine arrived at the police station. A dignified-looking man with a Western appearance but wearing full-on Sheik robes emerged and declared that he had information he'd like to impart.

I'd been up since dawn, had spoken to at least twenty people already that day. I was exhausted. So I let the guy wait while I took a short break. When I saw the robed man still sitting patiently a quarter of an hour later, smoking a Gauloises (the aroma only slightly pleasanter, I thought, than the burn pit), I figured this guy might have something worth listening to.

And did he ever.

"I am the hereditary Sheik of Saladin Province," he told me in excellent English. He'd brought along his papers to prove his centuries-old pedigree. As we spoke, I understood that he was a highly educated person of tremendous knowledge and influence, a banker with the Bank of Iraq, a living, breathing Who's Who of contacts and priceless inside information. He was the antidote to Baghdadi; he was not opaque, solemn, or burning with zealotry. He was worldly, charming, had an impish sense of humor and a twinkle in his eye, wore gold-rimmed glasses and was clean-shaven but for a mustache. When he showed me his papers, he cracked a joke: "You can see that I am no fake Sheik!" This was more than a play on words; it was known that Saddam had been dispensing the title of "Sheik" pretty freely to sycophants and loyalists, so there were, in fact, a lot of fake Sheiks running around. Our guy was definitely not one of those, and he made sure we knew it. And he was anything but blindly loyal to Saddam.

He was forthright and more than eager to talk on that first day I met him. I just listened, not daring to distract or interrupt. Here was a rich vein of live info, the sort intel agents dream of.

"I am the banker of the man who is Saddam Hussein's banker," he told me. "His name is Ali Sa'ad Hassan, but he is also known as Abu Seger;" (pronounced SAY-jer) "I know everything about his finances. You will be very interested in what you find in this man's house, which is only a couple of blocks from here."

Over more visits in subsequent days, the Sheik provided statements, papers, and evidence pertaining to Abu Seger. He told us of vast quantities of cash and gold shipped into Samarra. We began putting together a case and a plan to apprehend Abu Seger. And the Sheik and I were becoming fast friends. It was always a pleasure to see the black Mercedes pull up.

———————

Not everyone appearing at the police station arrived in a chauffeured limousine bearing crucial intelligence. Some came under cover of darkness and left nothing except memories of themselves I know I will never shake. Like the young woman in a burka, speaking perfect English, pushing her grandmother in a wheelchair.

"I am living in slavery," she said. "I do not want to live as a slave any longer." The grandmother never spoke, and I had no idea if she understood any English at all, but I could see by her expression and demeanor that she was totally on her granddaughter's side.

My American translator immediately offered the young woman a job as a translator.

"We want you to come to work right away," he said. The emotions chasing one another on the young woman's face while she considered this offer were complicated, ranging from joy to terror.

"Well, there might be a problem," she said. "I will have to go home first. I hope I can return tomorrow."

I walked her outside.

"I hope you come back. But please," I said, "be very, very careful. Don't do anything that might put you in danger." I could only imagine her home situation. A father, a husband, brothers? How well I knew what it was to live under the fist of a tyrannical patriarch.

When she left, it was with a sense of fatalism that I watched her push her grandmother's wheelchair beyond the glow of the streetlight. I kept my eyes on them until they vanished.

I never saw her again.

And a night or so later, well after dark, a girl, much younger, perhaps eleven, appeared at the station, alone. She wore a scarf on her head, her best shoes, a coat, and she was carrying a little suitcase.

"I need help," she said. "I want to leave. My father and uncles are making me do things I don't want to do."

Appalled, I brought her inside. But the moment she caught sight of the two Shia policemen, popping cashews into their mouths and eyeing her like jackals looking at a baby rabbit, she shrank back.

"I can't," she said. "I can't." And in the next moment she was out the door, hurrying into the darkness with her little suitcase.

Watching her disappear, I'd never felt quite so helpless.

She, too, I never saw again.

## CHAPTER 11

# WHO GOES THERE?

**A**nother person of great gravitas presented himself at the police station, arriving unannounced not long after our night with Al Baghdadi, but unlike the Sheik, he was not keen on making friends with me—nor I with him. He and I took a look at one another, and it was a look of mutual recognition, each of us saying to the other without words: *I know what you are. I can't trust you.*

His name was Mahmoud, he was in his fifties or early sixties, and he was a colonel with the Mukhabarat. He was friendly, casual, and charming, all of which put me on my guard instantly. The Sheik was all of those things, too, but unlike this man, he had not been a high-ranking officer in Saddam's intelligence organization—another way of saying highly experienced professional spy. Mahmoud and Baghdadi surely knew each other. It would not have surprised me to learn that Baghdadi sent him.

It was obvious that Mahmoud and the Sheik were acquainted, that each at the very least knew who the other was. How did I know? Because they carefully avoided one another if they both happened to be at the police station. They never spoke, and their eyes slid in the other direction if they happened to pass in the hall or on the steps. I didn't ask the Sheik about Mahmoud; I had a powerful sense of a tacit agreement between the Sheik and myself not to speak of Mahmoud, that there was possibly some sort of delicate behind-the-scenes equilibrium I'd best not disturb.

My colleagues Stavros, May, and Jason Richter (not his real name), all significantly younger than I was and lacking my training and experience in intelligence, formed a Mahmoud fan club right away. He had a distinctly non-Arab appearance. In size and coloring, he could easily have passed for European, and I could see that this was an attribute he emphasized and played up to great effect when cultivating (or, as I came to suspect, "recruiting") my teammates. He was big and paternal, naturally attractive to these young American agents on their first mission.

Stavros especially took a shine to Mahmoud. I have no doubt that Mahmoud's hyper-sensitive antennae picked up right away on Stavros' "abilities." I could imagine Mahmoud thinking to himself: *Hmmm. A man with a temper. This could be a useful weakness.*

One day a few weeks after he ingratiated himself with my team, I happened to walk in on a meeting they were holding with Mahmoud. I'd known about the meeting (to which I'd not been invited), but had been distracted by other business, and only decided to check in on them after the session was well underway. What I saw when I opened the door stunned me.

Stavros, May, and Richter (who was about 6'6") all sat cross-legged on the floor at the feet of Mahmoud, who'd settled himself in a big comfortable easy chair, holding court, guru-like, while the three Americans gazed up at him with what could only be called adulation.

I'd walked in on a snake-charming session. The first directive in intelligence is "asset control." *You* control the asset, you do not let the asset control *you*. In that room, Mahmoud was in complete control. You don't survive decades in the Mukhabarat and rise to high rank unless you're a master of intrigue. He plainly saw that the three young'uns he courted had zero experience in spy vs. spy, especially in an exotic culture, that they were juicy fish on his line that he had merely to reel in. He could play them any way he saw fit. I was, I was sure, witnessing an intelligence coup. Mahmoud glanced casually in my direction. The three turned closed faces to me; in that instant, *I* was the enemy. And Mahmoud, perspicacious devil, correctly read all of it, I have no doubt. *We've been penetrated,* I thought. *From this moment on, I can't trust my own team.* He saw me seeing; I saw him seeing me see; he knew that I knew that he knew. And all of this occurred in the space of a few seconds after I opened the door.

I came in and sat down. In a chair, not on the floor. He was smooth. He didn't break stride. He was in the middle of a sentence, and he went right on speaking.

". . . this goes hand in hand with what I'm saying . . ." He paused, while I wondered exactly what it was he'd been saying before I interrupted. ". . . about the massacre at Falluja," he continued.

*What?* Massacre at Falluja? This was the first I'd heard of a massacre. And he looked at me when he spoke his next words: "It's why you are going to be attacked. In retaliation. They are going to destroy your Abrams tank."

Our command had chosen not to inform us that on April 28, just a few days earlier, American soldiers, occupying a school building in Falluja, had fired on an unarmed crowd of protestors, killing seventeen people. The city was in an uproar. I learned about this disaster and the backlash of rage that followed not from my own people but from this career spy sitting comfortably in our midst. I did my best to contain my shock.

A few days earlier, the Sheik had warned us of an impending attack on the M-1 Abrams tank at our installation on the other side of the Tigris. He said a special tank-killing weapon would be used, unlike anything we'd ever seen. The tank was moved, and the attack did not materialize. Now, here at this meeting, Mahmoud was again warning us of an attack on the Abrams.

This time, very soon after Mahmoud's "meeting" with my team, the attack occurred. The tank was in motion, being driven at dusk across the dam spanning the Tigris, about a hundred yards from the police station. The projectile entered the tank like the proverbial hot knife into butter, destroying it, not by blowing it up but by travelling through its vital innards like a bullet going cleanly through a human body. The soldier driving the tank was obviously aware the tank had been hit, and thought at first that maybe he'd been grazed. He said later he'd felt his right leg itching; he looked down, and saw his severed leg lying on the floor.

The weapon that destroyed the multi-million-dollar, state-of-the-art, space-age-armored Abrams lodged itself in the tank's combat light, and so we were able to retrieve it. It was a spooky object: about the size of a pencil, with a blunt—not pointed—tip. The metal it was made of was described as "like nothing on earth." In doing BDA (Battle Damage Assessment), I examined the entrance hole: it was about the size of a quarter. We would learn the weapon's name: the Kornet Anti-tank Missile, made in Russia.

Mahmoud's correct prediction of an attack soon after the Sheik's predicted attack, which did not materialize, had a strong flavor of one-upmanship. *Listen to me, not to him*, he seemed to be saying. For all we knew, he had used his influence to stop the attack predicted by the Sheik in order to discredit him. He was, as they say in the spy business, establishing his bona fides. Not with me, though. His presence in our midst put me in mind of the hatchling cuckoo, which takes over other birds' nests and poses as one of them, reaping all sorts of benefits, to the hosts' considerable detriment.

In this case, the cuckoo in our nest was a master manipulator. He could not have been anything else and rise to longstanding prestige such as he had in the Mukhabarat. My teammates' chumminess with him was the tipping point in my distrust of them. I knew I could never rely on their judgment. Their vulnerability was on display, and we were in possible danger because of it.

Consider the milieu: Samarra right after the fall of Saddam teemed with volatile and ever-shifting alliances, rivalries, and enmities. The city was full of newly laid-off Sunni Republican Guard soldiers who had, until recently, been part of the highly privileged and well-paid "inner circle" surrounding Saddam, protecting him and doing his bidding. Now, of course, they were "unemployed" and not happy, especially with the Americans who put them out of their jobs by toppling Saddam. To them, we were anything but "liberators." They tried to blend in, but I was able to pick them out of the population; they tended to be bigger than anyone else, hand-chosen by Saddam for size and strength, and then fed and maintained very well. They had an aura of long-time entitlement about them, plus there was a sort of sideways glance we'd get from these out-of-work tough guys, a look of skulking resentment on their faces that they were unable to conceal.

The huge old cemetery in the middle of the city, maybe three or four thousand acres, had small but well-appointed sandstone houses around the perimeter. These houses had been bought by Saddam, and given to his Republican Guard guys in Samarra, another way to shore up their loyalty. If we found ourselves in conversation with largish men near these houses, chances were good we were in the presence of Saddam's ex-employees—who, of course, hated our guts but needed to keep a low profile now that the majority (and formerly oppressed) Shia were in ascendance.

And Samarra was the headquarters of the Ba'ath Party, nominally loyal to Saddam in this post-Saddam era, but in great disarray, its members of varying rank and varying loyalty to one another, and with countless personal scores to settle among themselves. Many Ba'ath Party members, now that Saddam was out, came and supplicated themselves to the Americans, badmouthing and implicating some of their compatriots, saying, in effect: *I'm a good guy, but this guy over here is a bad guy.* Mahmoud was, of course, a member of the Ba'ath Party.

With the advent of Mahmoud, my teammates—Stavros, May, and Richter—suddenly had a keen interest in the activities of the Ba'ath Party, to the exclusion of just about everything else. This struck me as fishy. It's well known that Saddam was a big admirer of Stalin. Stalin was big on intra-party purges, periodic housecleaning to get rid of annoying or otherwise unsatisfactory party members. And he wasn't kind and sensitive about it. Saddam emulated Stalin in many ways, and he was famous for removing troublesome party members violently and sadistically—as in the famous purge of 1979, where sixty-eight Ba'athists accused of treason were dragged out of an assembly, twenty-two of them tried and executed, and the ones not executed forced to fire the guns. Stalin would have been proud.

So here was this crafty Col. Mahmoud, surely seeing a golden opportunity to use an "overwhelming force"—in this case, us, the American occupiers—to do the dirty work of cleaning house in the post-Saddam Ba'ath Party. Name a name here, drop an insinuation there, settle old grudges, make strategic chess moves. Rat someone out, get him a one-way plane ticket to Guantanamo, a.k.a.

"Club Fed," compliments of the USA. This was what I suspected, deep in my bones. Also, in retrospect, I think that Mahmoud knew before we did that very soon there would be American-sponsored Shia Death squads in Samarra. Who better to assist in eliminating certain inconvenient Sunni Ba'athists, and to keep things stirred up and the fear level high? No, I didn't trust him. And just as deep in my bones, I trusted the Sheik. That trust would soon prove to be more than justified.

I could never confirm beyond doubt that Mahmoud was doing what I thought he was doing, but he did become a chronic lurking presence, contributing to the atmosphere of unease, paranoia, danger, and dissension within our ranks that we operated under, and which only increased as events unfolded.

About twenty-four hours after the attack on the Abrams, disaster struck, upping the ante exponentially. The cause was plain old cultural ignorance. Or was it?

I happened to be up on the roof of the police station. The sun was just going down, but there was plenty of daylight. The view was splendid; beyond the cemetery I could see the Golden Mosque to the west, and right in front of it, the Blue Mosque; to the east, the Spiral Mosque, and in front of that, the Garden of Allah. In the cemetery were countless crypts resembling miniature mosques. Ancient, timeless wonders standing sentry over busy modern lights, life, and traffic.

I watched an American foot patrol heading east on the street below, in formation, moving along calmly, headed in the direction of a traffic circle. And I saw, approaching the traffic circle from the south, a joyous, honking, headlight-flashing procession of cars and trucks, occasional volleys of gunfire—a wedding party!

The wedding party got into the traffic circle first, before the patrol reached it, and made a festive round. The foot patrol quickly found itself alongside the last vehicle in the procession: a pickup truck, with three very young men— teenagers, it would turn out—in the back, each carrying an AK-47. *Jesus,* I thought. *Please, everybody stay cool.*

In Iraq, everyone is armed. We think we have a lot of guns here in the United States, but we're flower children compared to Iraq, where the government freely handed out guns so citizens could defend against invaders. And guns are fired in celebration as often as in conflict. A party just isn't a party without the ear-splitting rat-a-tat of automatic weapons fired at the sky.

But the soldiers in the patrol who came up alongside that pickup saw armed young men in the back, guns pointed at the Americans. The soldiers fired.

"NO!" I yelled pointlessly. No one could hear me.

We'd quickly learn that all three Iraqi boys were killed instantly.

I knew there would be no coming back from this, and I was right. The bodies were brought to headquarters and laid out in a tent. Somehow, somebody photographed the bodies, and the pictures wound up on CNN. It was a catastrophe on every level, and, as I correctly predicted, a watershed moment. The father of two of the dead boys was a tribal warlord. He was wild with grief and fury, and declared jihad against the Americans.

Retribution was rapid and decisive.

That night, I was resting in the police station when I heard a motorbike outside rev and speed away. A few seconds later, a shuddering explosion cut the power and we were in total darkness. Mortar rounds followed almost immediately. I was in the back part of the building, and the mortars were hitting toward the front, but I could feel the concussions as they hit, seconds apart, the noise of each explosion filling the world. Windows shattered and screams pierced the night.

Then a soldier appeared, like a miner in a tunnel with the beam of light from his vest cutting through the blackness.

"Wounded in the courtyard!" he yelled. I fumbled for my helmet and medical kit and headed to the front. As I ran, I was aware of something sparking past my head, delivering a small punch to my face as it went. Whatever it was, it didn't stop me, so I just kept moving.

The patrol that had fired on the wedding party had returned. They were the target of the Iraqi gunners, who'd waited to attack until the patrol was in the courtyard and opening the doors of their vehicles. Six or seven of the ten vehicles in the patrol were on fire now. There was no other light except for the fire and the erratically crisscrossing beams from helmets and vests.

"Over here!" somebody yelled.

I went. A soldier lay in a shining red pool six feet across. I'd witnessed my share of gore, but never had I seen so much blood from one person. Expecting a mortar to hit at any moment, I knelt, my knees in the warm wet blood, its glistening expanse reflecting fire. He was breathing. *Artery,* I thought. *Only way there'd be this much blood. Femoral artery, I'm betting*, and I was right. The wound was just a small nick, but that's all it took.

Using my *keffiyah*, I tourniqueted him, my hands slippery with blood. Soon another medic was at my side, inserting an IV to give the guy fluids. We summoned an M-113 personnel carrier, loaded him in, and set off on a wild rumbling ride to the field station hospital on the other side of the river, a young soldier driving, me in the back with the wounded man, tending to him as best I could, unable to see anything going on outside. In the cramped, jostling darkness, with no illumination except for the dim red interior light, I was making medical decisions that would have been tricky in a calm room under fluorescent bulbs. When you're administering an IV and the patient is tourniqueted, you have to take care that the fluid doesn't enter the vein with too much pressure, or you might blow the clot. So you adjust, compensate, tighten, loosen, all the while attending to breathing and heartbeat. Imagine doing that in a dim, jouncing, swerving, roaring, rolling metal box under fire.

The mortar rounds followed us down the road like the footsteps of some malevolent giant, hitting just behind us, sending the M-113 skidding this way and that as if we were sliding on ice. The kid at the wheel did a superb job, drove that huge clunky heavy machine like Mario Andretti, dodging, compensating, accelerating, braking, and keeping a cool, fearless head. He got us to the field station in one piece. The wounded sergeant survived, but just barely. The attack that wounded him so grievously was instant payback for the young men killed in the wedding procession earlier in that long, long night.

I'd find out some details later. One of the soldiers in the patrol told me that the boys, when they saw the Americans alongside them, had raised their weapons and pointed them at the soldiers. Or at least, that's what it looked like. The boys in the pickup didn't fire, but the soldiers did.

The lethal mishap was quickly attributed to an unfortunate misunderstanding brought about by lack of knowledge of local customs. Certainly possible. But just to give you an idea of the potent malignance of Mahmoud's presence, a darker idea cast a shadow in my own mind: Had Mahmoud, the master of provocation, with his intimate knowledge of the dynamics of violence, perhaps made a suggestion to the fifteen-year-old wedding-party boys before the festivities? Salute the Americans with your guns. They will see it as a gesture of camaraderie. They will respect you if they think you are tough guys.

Or some such, knowing full well how the Americans would react, that the boys would be mowed down, and the people would howl for vengeance, that they'd turn on the Americans for good, that chaos would erupt. Why, you ask, might he want to foment such strife, with so much collateral damage to everyday Iraqis? Simple: violence and chaos with some human sacrifice in the mix are the raw materials out of which a savvy operator might further an ultimate agenda—promote power for himself and his cohort. Just think Machiavelli.

Later, when I was no longer in Iraq, and I was in touch with various federal and military policing agencies, I'd hear Mahmoud's name spoken again, in a context that would justify my suspicions.

The day after the attack, after a night of zero sleep, when I finally had time to stop and assess, I looked at my haggard face in a mirror. I found that I had some shrapnel in my cheek and that part of my right earlobe was missing. I recalled the sparks whizzing by the night before as I headed out to the courtyard, the slight punch to the kisser. A little difference in trajectory, I realized, and my entire head might have been missing.

*So much for good will,* I thought. The tide had turned with a vengeance. And that was only the beginning.

———

I took a short trip down to Balad not long after. It was a ride of only an hour or so, and though I'd at first been happy to leave Balad behind, now I was glad to go down there occasionally and get away for a few hours from the chronic strife in Samarra, both within the police station and out in the city. Since the wedding massacre, as we came to call it, we were diving for cover just about every night. Many of the rocket and mortar attacks were fired from the huge old cemetery behind us; the endless rows of stones and mausoleums provided excellent cover.

Occasionally, we were lulled into thinking things had simmered down, that maybe we'd get a break. Like the night I stepped outside up on the roof to escape the oppressive heat of the police station. Things had been quiet. The sky was the deep indigo fading into black you see just before full darkness falls, a crescent moon riding high, attended by a couple of brilliant points of light, planets, and stars.

I marveled, as always, at the vision of the Golden Mosque, part of the Al Askari Shrine, one of the holiest sites anywhere in the Muslim world, now shining in the pale glow of the moon. For a moment, all was timeless, serene. I expected to see a turbaned genie riding a magic carpet.

The reverie was short-lived: in the next moment, a rocket arced over the top of the mosque, hit the ground beyond, and tracer fire was returned.

With the increased attacks, my own people were responding exactly as they should not have if they'd had a lick of sense: with more detainment and ever-rougher treatment of detainees.

Thus the age-old human tendency of reciprocal retribution was spiraling out of control. I complained to my command regularly.

I reminded them that the Americans had invaded the Iraqis' country, and were now torturing and killing them and their kids. We're surrounded by angry people, I said, who know our habits, our weaknesses, are watching our every move, and know exactly how, when, and where to take us out. They have the weapons to do it, and the experience, from fighting the Iranians for eight long bloody years, not to mention living under Saddam's boot heel forever. They're way, way tougher than we are, and they are not afraid to die. They're gonna pulverize us if we don't cool it.

My complaints went into the usual deep well of oblivion. The situation deteriorated around us daily. And that's how a quick trip to Balad came to seem like a mini-vacation, and how I came to be there on the same day a VIP arrived.

I was in the communications shack near the runway. I sat at a desk, computer screen in front of me, checking messages from home, when Maloney came in, escorting a tall, aviator-glasses-wearing officer fresh off an incoming flight.

In the same way Baghdaddi looked like every American's fever dream of a terrorist, this customer looked like every American's fondest fantasy of a rugged, square-jawed military guy—craggy, steely, spit-shined, complete with silver-gray buzzcut.

I recognized him even before his name tag confirmed who he was: Major General Geoffrey Miller, commander of Guantanamo since 2002. He had plenty of what we call "command presence;" Maloney scurried around him like an eager terrier around a Great Dane.

I seemed to be the only one aside from Maloney who knew who he was. Miller and I had a tacit exchange: he saw me look up from the computer, saw me recognizing him, and saw me getting ready to stand, as you do when an officer enters. He signaled me to stay seated, so I did.

Military insignia are instantly readable to those in the know. I saw the two stars of a major general, and the crossed bars of an artillery specialist. What I did not see on the chest of this chap who had surely come to Iraq on a special intel mission was the distinctive but discreet rose-and-helios pin of military intelligence.

And I heard these words spoken by him, loud and clear, still resonating in my memory:

"I'm here to Gitmo-ize Abu Ghraib."

# CHAPTER 12

# HELL TO PAY

From an inner room of the police station, Stavros could be heard screaming and cursing, and occasionally the pictures on our side of the wall jumped as a body on the other side was slammed against the cement brick. I and some others, including two transport guys, were in the front office. I saw the people at their computers visibly flinch with each blow, but they did not move their eyes from their screens and they continued to type. One of the transport guys, less accustomed to ignoring a nearby beating, looked at us.

"Why are you doing this?"

I sighed. "That's just Stavros."

As more and more detainees were brought by the MPs to the police station, I saw more and more of them arriving in seriously roughed-up condition. One of my jobs as medic was to evaluate each prisoner and fill out a detailed three-part medical report for each one: history, diagnosis, and treatment. I duly sent the reports on to Balad, and I kept copies. I would eventually accumulate fifty-two of these reports. Beaten up during capture and transit, men and boys were arriving with bloody heads, cuts, bruises, and contusions. For some, that was a mere taste of what was to come when they were delivered to the "liberators" for questioning. My reports often included complaints about my own colleagues, and injuries sustained by the detainees at their hands.

Stavros, who had let it be known that he held a special hatred in his heart for Arabs for perceived historic crimes against Greeks, did his favorite style of "interrogation" there at the police station, turning himself loose to exact revenge for ancient grievances. Stavros quickly got tired of me warning him that this was bad policy, stupid, and dangerous, especially in the wake of the public-relations disaster of the wedding day massacre. You're living up to their worst ideas about us, I told him. And you're sabotaging our work here, which is to gather useful intelligence. Beating the crap out of people accomplishes nothing except making them hate us.

Stavros especially was resistant to reason. I believed I saw Mahmoud's fingerprints on this upsurge in violence and abuse. The Mukhabarat were not known for their kindly, enlightened treatment of prisoners; their fearsome rep for ruthlessness included extreme torture. I couldn't help but think that Stavros in particular was getting tips, suggestions, and encouragement from Mahmoud, who recognized Stavros' innate aptitude, and would have his own reasons for keeping the pot stirred.

The transport guy said he was aware of Stavros' reputation, but what he said next was a revelation and a harbinger of what would eventually break as the news story heard 'round the world:

"Do you know what they're doing in Abu Ghraib right now? They're destroying these guys. You should come down and see for yourself."

This was multi-layered bad news for me. I'd treated a lot of beaten-up prisoners after interrogations, and when writing up their medical reports, cited the abuse emphatically, then released them to be possibly sent to Abu Ghraib. Had I been unwittingly sending them back into hell? I knew I'd have to go. My conscience would eat me alive if I didn't.

This wasn't my first whiff of bad news about Abu Ghraib. Geoffrey Miller's colorful words still echoed, and not long before, on a trip to Beled (not Balad), I'd met an officer named Nate Sassaman, who would later become notorious for his part in a cover-up of the drowning death of one of two young Iraqi brothers, seized by Sassaman's men for a curfew violation and forced by the soldiers to jump off a bridge into the Tigris. One made it out of the river, the other didn't.

When I met him in Beled, Sassaman was already under investigation for teaching the grunts under his command at Samarra how to lie effectively to the CID (Criminal Investigations Department). He was smart, a smooth operator, high achiever, and well-known hard-ass, in charge of controlling and disciplining, very effectively, the increasingly pissed-off local Sunni population. On that day, I and a few others stood with Sassaman and watched a group of Iraqi prisoners doing exercises. The scene was relatively civilized. The prisoners didn't look particularly miserable, mistreated, or angry.

Sassaman laughed. "The joke's on them," he said with a smirk.

"What do you mean?" I asked.

"They don't know it, but tomorrow they're off to Abu Ghraib. They'd be acting a whole lot different if they knew." What this meant, of course, was that though the lid was months away from being blown off, and the worst was yet to come, Abu Ghraib under the Americans already had a grim reputation among those in the know.

I rode down with the next transport. My concern for the prisoners was top priority, of course, but I had other reasons to go to Abu Ghraib.

Not only had I been a corrections officer at Folsom for many years, but I had a pretty extensive background in how prisons work. Most people believe that what they've seen in movies and on television makes them experts on prisons. Maybe you saw Sylvester Stallone in *Lockup* or Morgan Freeman in *Shawshank Redemption* and think you're knowledgeable about maximum-security prisons. That's like believing that you know all about interstellar travel because you watched *Star Trek*.

Folsom, which was the only "Level 4" (maximum security) prison outside of Federal lockups until Pelican Bay came into existence, is a serious place. It was the only non-Federal pen until then that had a SHU, the dreaded Security Housing Unit, better known as solitary confinement. Much of the population at Folsom when I was there was hardcore, violent, and recidivistic, and many of them had little left to lose. Gangs were rife, at bloody war with each other and the world.

During my time at Folsom, as I mentioned earlier, I helped develop a computer program called the Violence Management Plan, designed to track lines of communication among prisoners, the objective being to cut down on gangs, fighting, knifings, and riots.

For such a worldly person as I believe myself to be, my own naiveté sometimes startles me. Here's a lesson I eventually learned: the prison authorities don't actually want to end prison violence. To them, it's a resource, to be conserved and exploited. Cultivated and properly contained, measured eruptions of violence among prisoners can be an invaluable tool allowing the authorities to stay in control through violent, oppressive response. Surprise!

When I made my first trip to Abu Ghraib, I was still laboring under the illusion that the Folsom Violence Management Program might be of interest to those in charge. I wanted to see the place, get a feel for how it was run, and perhaps even make some constructive suggestions.

I didn't ask anyone's permission to go, least of all that of Maloney and Segura, who, I knew, didn't want me anywhere near Abu Ghraib. I was already known as a "troublemaker," having complained about the crude interrogation techniques of my colleagues, Stavros in particular, and the lack of remedial action on the part of my command. So I made an executive decision in my capacity as intelligence agent and medic, and simply went. I had to leave Stavros, May, and Richter in charge, which I wasn't happy about, but this was a trip I had to make. Stavros was happy to see me go. A whole day of no wet blanket wrecking his fun! And who knew—maybe I'd catch a bullet or mortar along the way!

The highway from Samarra down to greater Baghdad is not what you'd call scenic. The terrain is flat, dry, ugly, and monotonous and there's surprisingly little traffic even though it's a main artery. That part of the trip is relatively safe, so you might just feel bored and sleepy for the first couple of hours. But then you make a turn near Baghdad International Airport and head west toward Abu Ghraib and Fallujah on the road picturesquely nicknamed Death Alley. If we were going to get hit, that's where it was most likely to happen. We passed wrecked, overturned, bullet-riddled, and blown-up vehicles all along the way. By the time we arrived at Abu Ghraib after maybe a half hour on Death Alley, we were wide awake, jumpy, and hypervigilant, not to mention soaked in clammy sweat.

When Abu Ghraib was in view in the distance, its general outline was familiar to me. It looked like many modern US prisons, including the new Folsom, built by a California contracting company called Tutor-Saliba, formed in the 1950s, who specialize in big civil and industrial construction projects—airports, subways, stadiums, and yes, prisons. Abu Ghraib was built in the mid-1960s by British engineers using American blueprints, and it appeared to be typical Tutor-Saliba: two-story, sprawling, festoons of razor-wire, with a pentagon shape for high security, and guard towers. It made sense: the mid-'60s was honeymoon time for Saddam and his American sponsors—or, to be more accurate, his American employers. I don't know for a fact that Abu Ghraib was a Tutor-Saliba prison, but it sure looked like one to me, a likely early example of a huge American company getting a juicily lucrative contract in Iraq through the US government and making big bucks off of human misery.

We went through the sallyport (prisonese for main gate checkpoint), where every vehicle entering and everyone in it is counted and inspected for papers, weapons, explosives, and so forth. The series of high-security doors and gates we went through as we entered the prison were typical and familiar, too. Once we were inside, another powerful familiarity hit me in the face: the smell.

Wherever multitudes of humans cohabit, there will be a smell. But the smell of a prison is distinct: old food, unwashed bodies, and latrines, all with an acrid accent of anger exuded from the skin and sweat glands of thousands of mostly male people. The Abu Ghraib bouquet was a lot like the Folsom bouquet, but stronger, with a slightly exotic edge. But if I'd been brought there blindfolded (or with a bag over my head) I'd have instantly identified the aroma: *prison*. There was no mistaking it.

The next impression I got when we'd gone through all the gates and doors and were in the "release and receiving" area was that those in charge—the 372nd MP Company—didn't have the remotest idea of what they were doing. Trained to support combat operations, its members were mostly young and probably not trained to be prison guards or administrators, though a few individual members had, by chance, actually done stints as prison guards. The 372nd had been sent to Abu Ghraib shortly after the Americans had seized the prison, and when they got there, they were informed that they were now guards and pretty much left to figure things out for themselves. Presiding over them was Col. Thomas Pappas, who made his debut there by ordering HUEY military helicopters to hover low over the tents in the courtyard where a small city's worth of prisoners were housed. The violent hundred-mile-per-hour wind made by the huge rotors at close range destroyed and scattered tents, blankets, and possessions, which were all torn apart and sent flying in a roaring tornado.

Asked why he'd done it, Pappas had said: "To show 'em who's boss."

Right. Great diplomacy, there, Colonel.

Running a prison is seriously complicated. It takes experience, order, hierarchy, expertise, and smoothly interlocking logistics. You're feeding, moving, and controlling hundreds of unhappy people at a time, in separate groups, keeping track of why they are there, who they are, where they are, and where they are going. Various groups must be segregated at all times from certain other groups. I could see that some of the smarter kids—and I call them kids because that's what they were, a full generation younger than I was—were making an effort to grow into this enormous, crazy responsibility that had been thrust on them. But for most of this crew, it was hopeless, as if they were running some combination of frat house and boot camp.

Add to the mix that they were scared. Abu Ghraib was a dark, remote, ugly place with a history of cruelty and violence that just about oozed from the walls; now, with the Americans in charge, it was the most-attacked US-held position in Iraq. There were assaults every day: bullets, grenades, mortars, and rockets. On top of that, living conditions for the soldiers were piss-poor, to put it politely. When the Americans invaded, Saddam had opened the gates of Abu Ghraib. The prisoners fled. The emptied-out prison was found to be in a state of advanced dereliction and decay: filthy water, broken plumbing, raw sewage, no power, stinking refuse dumps, feral dogs feeding on garbage, and worse. The soldiers were quartered in cells inside the building. Between the fear, the chaos, and the accommodations, no wonder morale was bad. I recognized faces; the last time I'd seen some of these nineteen- or twenty- or twenty-two-year-olds was in Kuwait and had thought at the time that the military had ill-prepared them for war. Now here they were, in conditions that would have tried even the most hardened veterans.

The interior layout was Folsom-like, too. There were two stories, tiers of cells, a double staircase at each end of a block, and hallways radiating outward from a central hub, all familiar. It was a long walk from R&R to Building 1-A, the highest security wing, where the prisoners I was there to check on were being kept, whether they merited such hardcore classification or not. Along the way, I saw overcrowding (though nothing like what was to come) and chaos. I saw piles of debris. But according to the transport sergeant accompanying me, conditions were way better than when he'd first arrived a few weeks before.

"See all these hallways here?" he said, indicating the radiating corridors. "It was like looking into the mouth of hell. The power was out, so there was hardly any light during the day and none at all at night. You could smell rotting bodies down those halls. If you shined a light in there, the eyes of rats and dogs feeding on corpses flashed back at you. That's how it was when we took over."

The rotting human flesh and scavenging dogs were gone by the time I got there, and power had been restored, but there were still piles of broken cement, twisted metal, and shattered glass. I saw execution rooms with hooks and scaffolds. Folsom had an execution room, but only one. Here, there were many.

"And the central courtyard," said the sergeant. "There was a big hole there where Saddam dumped executed prisoners. A mass grave right in the middle of everything. Dogs trotting around carrying human bones." He looked at me and shook his head. "Talk about bad vibes."

Bad vibes, indeed. A squirmy nightmare of a grade-Z horror movie, but real. And I asked myself: why would the American military choose to set themselves up in one of the most infamous stockades in the Middle East, a place with a decades-long history of blood, pain, and death, and famous for it? The Americans would now be indelibly associated in the popular Iraqi mind with this legendary pit of misery, and we'd be bound to replicate some of that misery. To my mind, it was just setting ourselves up for tragedy, catastrophe. If there are ghosts, this place had to be swarming with them.

And then bring in a bunch of fresh-faced kids to run things and make life-and-death decisions, while supervised by only a handful of corrupt officers? An answer to my question was tentatively forming in my mind, and it was not much to my liking. None of this was accidental. It was quite possibly all purposely and premeditatedly planned. Years later, I'd read an essay written by an

Arab journalist during the run-up to the war. In this piece, the writer said that the purpose of the American invasion, the current one and past ones, in both Iraq and Afghanistan and elsewhere, was to "cauldronize" the Middle East, reduce it to a state of malleable chaos, thus making it ripe for corporate colonization and exploitation. Any other ostensible justification for invasion— payback for 9/11, for instance—was an elaborate façade, an advertising campaign specifically designed to package and sell the war to the American people.

Remember what I said about prison authorities not actually wanting to end violence within the walls? That the chaos was useful to them? It's a similar phenomenon to that cauldronization, and a component of it: the cultivation of violence and chaos in order to justify certain ends (think Mahmoud). What ends, you ask? In the case of Abu Ghraib, to ensure that the war would go on and on, though at the time of this visit to Abu Ghraib I was many months away from putting it all together in my mind. I could not have known it then, but some harsh lessons lay in my immediate future that would bring it all into clarity and focus.

But before my visit that day was over, any hifalutin notions I might have had about making suggestions based on my Folsom experience already seemed absurd. The place was just in too much chaos.

I was there to see for myself whether prisoners were being "destroyed," as the transport guy had put it. I confess that on that particular day I did not see anything alarmingly extreme. I saw prisoners with bags on their heads getting shoved around and yelled at by American soldiers. I didn't see anyone on the floor with a boot on his neck, and I didn't see anyone in stress positions. I got a strong impression that the Iraqi prisoners had not yet caught on to how little we were actually in control; they were in Abu Ghraib, which Saddam had run with utmost iron cruelty for decades, and were conditioned to expect instant, lethal, and brutal response to any kind of disobedience.

I had a powerful sense, though, that the situation was tenuous. All the ingredients for potential disaster were present, just a breath away from ignition, like a pile of bone-dry brush just waiting for somebody to flick a cigarette onto it.

When we got to 1-A, I saw immediately that it was swarming with CIA types passing as grunts and guards. Though they wore the same camo as the rest of us, they had mannerisms and quirks they could not hide from a trained eye. To me, they stood out as if they had blinking neon signs on their backs. The place was thoroughly infiltrated.

One of the most vivid memories I have from Abu Ghraib was of an officer, sitting in a side room inside 1-A, watching an interrogation through one-way glass. The transport sergeant said to me: "That's the big guy himself. That's Col. Larry James."

I didn't know the full significance of this sighting at the time, nor did I know what I would later know about Dr. Larry James, that he would become notorious as the licensed psychologist who lent his expertise to the fine-tuning of torture via mental, emotional, and psychological manipulation. He would later claim that his purpose was to oversee interrogations and mitigate unnecessary cruelty, but many who watched him at work said that his methods, though technically bloodless, were insidiously abusive, including tactics like prolonged solitary confinement for new detainees in order to "enhance and exploit their disorientation."

He started out at Guantanamo, and witnesses would say that during his time there, the usual crude stuff went on uninterrupted—beatings, rape threats, painful positions, and sexual humiliation. His job, whether he admitted it to himself or anybody else, was to justify the "ethics" of this or that torture practice. He did not officially bring his "expertise" to Abu Ghraib until 2004, after the huge scandal broke—but he was there on that day in May of 2003 when I was there. I saw him with my own eyes.

So, here was another alumnus of Guantanamo, assisting in the "Gitmo-ization" of Abu Ghraib—meaning, in part, as we would learn, the use of MPs to "soften up" detainees for interrogation. On this day, he sat and watched an interrogation with cool detachment. I remember thinking: *Well, for torture, this is certainly nonchalant.* No one was screaming. No bodies were being slammed against a wall. Perhaps he was observing a phase of prolonged sleep deprivation. Perhaps he was taking notes, deciding what was "legal" and what was not. He looked pensive and professional, but I'm sure Dr. Mengele looked that way too when he was at his desk deep in thought.

I went back to Samarra not exactly reassured, but not in a state of acute alarm, either. I guess I was relieved that I didn't see anything I'd have to report.

Not long after, far, far from Iraq, I'd be talking about Abu Ghraib to a fellow service member who'd been there at about the same time. I described what I'd seen on that visit, how things didn't seem too dire, and how I'd come away with a conscience I could live with.

"Yeah," he said. "That's because you were there during the day." He paused. "It was a whole other world at night."

As it happened, I would go back to Abu Ghraib before long. This time, it would be personal, and I'd see for myself what could happen behind closed doors, away from the light of day. And my conscience would be anything but free and clear.

Capt. Segura, meantime, made himself directly complicit in the ongoing abuse back in Samarra. During one of Stavros's "interrogations," a louder, even more violent one than usual, I was standing outside the station with Segura and his sidekick-cum-bodyguard and old acquaintance of mine, 1st Sgt. Padilla, the two of them up from Balad for the day. All of us could hear from within Stavros bellowing like some crazed psycho. It was so loud that a gunner on guard duty up on the roof glared down at us.

"What the hell's going on in there?" the guy yelled. To my disgust, Segura gave me a warning look and yelled back:

"Nothing. We're dealing with it. It's okay."

———

What were we saying about nighttime being a whole other world, when the worst horrors seem to materialize?

At about 3 a.m. a few days later, I was sleeping the dead sleep of exhaustion in the airless room I shared with four others in the back of the police station when I was shaken out of my murky dreams.

"Doc, get up. You gotta see this. Bring your bag. Hurry. Main gate."

I rose from the egg-crate foam atop my cot, the depressions in the pad sloshing with sweat, grabbed my medical kit, and headed outside.

A young Arab man stood in a circle of gaping, speechless soldiers. In the weird malarial glow of the mercury-vapor lights, it took a moment for me to understand what I was seeing: the man had no arms. They'd been severed just below the shoulders. He was coated with blood. He fixed me with his eyes and crumpled to the ground.

I quickly knelt, put a finger on his carotid artery, and felt the final beats of his heart as the blood pumped out of him in rhythmic spurts. There was nothing I could do. I looked at the stumps: *What could have done this? A chainsaw?* More important: *Who* did this?

Only later did I learn of the presence of Shia death squads in Samarra intended to counter the growing Sunni insurgency. They were organized by a shadowy figure connected to Gen. David Petraeus and also to John Negroponte: retired Colonel James Steele, a.k.a. the Butcher of Latin America. He made his name in El Salvador in the early '80s as head of a US group of special forces dispatched by Ronald Reagan to train and fund the Salvadoran military to quash the guerilla uprising against the country's brutal right-wing regime. Steele's specialty had been the formation and training of Salvadoran death squads, the mere mention of which would eventually loosen bowels the world over, so fearsome was their reputation. The country was quickly plunged into civil war, death, and misery on a sickening scale. They say you're known by the company you keep; Steele was close pals with Roberto D'Aubuisson, a.k.a. "Blowtorch Bob," a School of the Americas alumnus and powerful right-wing Salvadoran politician.

In case you're not familiar with it: the School of the Americas is described euphemistically as ". . . a United States Department of Defense Institute that provides military training to government personnel in US-allied Latin American nations." More concisely, the SOA, established in Panama in 1946, has trained many thousands of Latin American soldiers over the decades in "counterinsurgency techniques." These "techniques" include sniper training, interrogation, torture, and psychological warfare. These lethal skills are used exclusively against the civilians of the countries in question, specifically those working to improve the lives of the poor and disenfranchised—educators, union organizers, nuns and priests, student leaders and such who would challenge US-supported strongmen.

Hundreds of thousands of Latin Americans have been tortured, "disappeared," raped, assassinated, and massacred by SOA alumni, whose job it is to prop up right-wing dictatorships. Kicked out of Panama in 1984, it relocated to Fort Benning, GA, with a fresh new name: the Western Hemisphere Institute for Security Cooperation (WHINSEC). Don't be fooled, though; it's the same old School of Assassins—oops, I mean School of the Americas—up to its old tricks. Your tax dollars at work.

Blowtorch Bob, like his buddy Steele, was a major death squad enthusiast. Think of the "bonding" between these two! Bob had been an interrogator for the Salvadoran military, during which time he earned his colorful moniker. It's not hard to imagine how.

Steele subsequently got caught in some Iran-Contra hanky-panky and "retired." But he had plenty of admirers; he was officially a civilian when, in 2003, at the behest of Cheney and Rumsfeld, he brought his expertise to Iraq.

The presence of these death squads and Steele's presence in Iraq while I was at Samarra was not made known to me or my intel unit, adding to the danger we were already in. What I saw that night, the man whose arms had been chainsawed off, was an early manifestation of a carefully calculated, highly cynical plan to inflame the ancient Sunni-Shia schism, which had, as I've mentioned, been more or less dormant (or at least tightly controlled) under Saddam's rule. Anyone would have thought that peace was the last thing the American command actually wanted. Or what certain factions of the post-Saddam Iraqi power structure wanted. I thought of Mahmoud, sitting like a pasha in the police station, dripping avuncular charm.

Pervasive cynicism seemed to extend its insidious tentacles disastrously. I traveled one day soon after to the nearby town of Beled (not to be confused with Balad) where there was a recently established American base.

Along the way, I came across possibly the most beautiful holy building I'd yet seen in Iraq, surpassing even the wonders in Samarra. It resembled a smaller Taj Mahal, complete with onion dome and graceful minarets. It was made of bright yellow brick inlaid with turquoise cloisonné. It was literally in the middle of nowhere. There was no time to stop and go inside, but I had my translator tell the one man in attendance that I was dazzled and in awe. This made the attendant glow with happiness. I carried that glow with me to Beled. That good feeling would soon be shattered. I'm grateful, though, that I saw that lonely sacred place before I saw what I was about to see.

We arrived. I was in a conversation with a major. We were there to explore the idea of setting up an intelligence collection effort involving dialogue with people at the local hospitals. Around us as we talked, personnel went about their business on an unremarkable day, walking and conversing, at ease. One soldier sat in a folding chair outside his tent, reading, perhaps twenty feet from where I and the major stood.

A single deafening BOOM nearly lifted us off the ground. The soldier in the chair had pulled out his 9 mm. pistol, and with zero warning, shot himself in the head. Others rushed toward him, but I didn't. I could see from where I was that there was nothing to be done. And though the report from the pistol as the soldier blew himself away took me by surprise, the act itself did not; it seemed altogether congruous with this perverse war. I recalled my wolf pal out in the desert looking into my eyes.

The bad omens were piling up like unpaid bills.

# CHAPTER 13

# NEIGHBORS

About twenty fierce-looking, very young Arab men surrounded, in a worshipful sort of way, five or six much older men sitting in a circle on a lush carpet. The older guys looked to be in their seventies, and wore full-on robes of office of the sort associated with Saudi Arabia, plus headdresses and curve-toed embroidered slippers. The younger guys wore dish-dash and radiated the devotion of acolytes plus an unalloyed sort of hatred for us Americans, hatred that I sensed was kept in check only by the presence of the older men. *All it would take,* I thought, *would be the smallest signal from these elders and we'd be torn apart in an instant.* I could just about smell the animal fear coming off my poor young Iraqi translator.

I was scared, too, but I stayed calm, pleasant, and diplomatic, for my own sake as much as everyone else's. I was introduced as "the doctor," which helped soften the general attitude a little. One of these older guys seemed to be the leader, and he invited me, in pretty good English, to sit down with them. Now I could see that this guy was a cleric, an imam.

Looking at him, I thought: *Damn. I've seen you somewhere before. But where?*

About five minutes earlier, a guy from the PSYOPS (Psychological Warfare) unit had hurried into the police station looking for me. He wasn't exactly sweating bullets, but it was obvious that he didn't want to waste any time.

"Doc, come on with us to the hospital building next door. Somebody's just moved in. We need to check it out."

Somebody? That word got my attention.

It was barely a minute's walk from the police station to the hospital, but in that interval it was clear that the locals knew something about who these new neighbors were. People tensed up visibly as I and my crew, fully armed, were seen traversing the thirty or forty feet to the door. The building was no longer a hospital, but it was far from abandoned.

I accepted the offer to sit, a little awkwardly, laden as I was with gear and weapons. I did my best to maintain my relaxed demeanor, hoping it would be contagious.

"We're not here to make trouble," I said, holding my hands palms-up in what I hoped was a universal gesture of peace. "We're here because we've been ordered to be here, but we'd rather not be here, and we want to go home as soon as we can."

The tension relaxed a notch or so when I spoke these words and my translator repeated them in Arabic, though he himself was still rigid with fear. His voice shook so that everyone could hear his terror. I felt very, very bad for him, for putting him in a situation like this, and rested a reassuring hand on his shoulder, though he jumped visibly before he realized whose hand it was. This small human gesture, and the translator's very human response, had a slight but definite further softening effect, especially among the elders.

I learned something about who these people were. The former hospital building was now a *madrassa* (Islamic religious school), and these guys had come in from Mecca with trucks full of medical supplies.

The familiar-looking older man stood and offered me a tour. The two of us left the others and strolled around the halls. The place had been thoroughly looted of any useful medical equipment.

"I'd like to show you something," said the man, taking me to the back of the building. We approached a doorless store room. "You may be able to help us. Perhaps you could look in there and tell me what you think."

I glanced into the room. A surge of adrenaline lurched through my body before my mind had time to fully comprehend the sight before my eyes: racks of 500-lb. bombs, at least ten of them, probably more, their nose-cones where the detonators resided pointing outward into the room, the seals on the nose-cones that contained the detonators ruptured in the 120-degree heat so that they oozed an evil-looking clear fluorescent-green fluid that resembled antifreeze and had already accumulated on the floor to a depth of three inches or so, covering it entirely. Big drops still fell from the nose-cones, hitting the pool on the floor with an audible hiss. At any moment, the whole works could have exploded sky-high. I jerked backward in shock.

My robed companion seemed highly amused at my reaction. The two of us hustled away while I promised to bring in a special crew to dispose of the lethal mess. As we hurried down the hall, the man put his hand on the knob of another door. "Here is something else I want you to see," he said.

*Christ, more bombs?* I thought, and braced myself. But there were no bombs. Instead, there was a stash of fine Persian rugs, leather ottomans, objets-d'art, and other furniture, lamps, and appointments. "Please," said the man. "Help yourself."

Bidding a hasty farewell, I got my people out of there fast and then made the promised arrangements to bring in an EOD (Explosive Ordnance Disposal) team ASAP. They arrived within a half-hour, pumped the room full of a special foam that filled every nook and displaced the oxygen, and proceeded with the successful neutralization and removal of the bombs. If the bombs had gone off, there would have been total death and destruction for a radius of a half-mile, at the least. It was a damned miracle that in the midst of the frequent mortar fire in recent weeks, the bombs had not been hit and set off.

Later, when the coast was clear, I went back and took the furniture and rugs I'd been offered, getting curious looks from people in the street as I and a couple of helpers carried the goodies back to the police station. I was able to make my office just a tad more homey and comfy. This was not merely pleasant for me, but would, I thought, help those who came in to speak to me feel a bit more relaxed. Among the items I "inherited" was an exquisite antique wooden rocking-camel, probably a hundred years old, plus a handsome camel-hide sofa. I had a little fantasy about how I might ship that rocking-camel home eventually, though I knew it was not just impossible but highly unethical.

While I was pleasurably arranging the furnishings, thinking about what the new arrivals had told me about coming in from Mecca, an associative switch clicked in my mind. Mecca! It came to me with an unpleasant jolt where I'd seen the genteel man whose largesse I was enjoying: on an undercover video I'd seen sometime during my intel training back home, made at the Kabaa (the big black stone at the center of the gargantuan al-Masjid al-Haram mosque in Mecca), around which countless thousands of Muslims swirl and pray every year during the hajj, a sacred pilgrimage.

In the video, the man had stood in front of the Kabaa, jabbing the air with his finger, ranting about how Jews are pigs and the Americans are their trained monkeys, and so on. Quite a different persona from that of the calm, civilized gent I encountered at the hospital. I never learned his name.

I was grateful for my delayed recognition of this fellow. If it had happened while I was face to face with him, would I have been able to disguise the flicker of realization? What might this guy have done if he'd seen me recognize him? As it was, I had what they call "plausible deniability."

That evening, the Sheik dropped by. He sat on the camel-hide sofa, ran an appraising hand along it, and lit a Gauloises while I finished writing up the day's long, long report.

"So," the Sheik said finally. "You met your new neighbors today."

I looked up, surprised.

"Oh? How did you find out?"

The Sheik laughed.

"The whole city is talking about it."

"What are you going to tell me?"

"Well," he said, looking at me and cocking his head waggishly, "this afternoon, when I heard that you got out of there alive, I was impressed."

He paused, exhaled an eloquent plume of smoke, and then spoke words that sent a *frisson* along my spine.

"Have you ever heard of Al Qaeda?"

This was only the second time I had heard those syllables uttered since I arrived in Iraq. The other time had been when the colonel who showed me the WMD used the phrase to refer to the air base.

This is notable for the reason that until we came and removed Saddam, Al Qaeda had not been much of a presence in Iraq, because Saddam had kept them under strict control. Now, here, only a few short weeks after the invasion, was the early manifestation of a significant "blossoming" by the organization the Americans had falsely told the world was headquartered in Iraq and in cahoots with Saddam.

The lie, of course, had been cooked up to justify the invasion and sold to the American people and the world as "payback" for 9/11. The invasion, the vacuum left after Saddam's removal, the growing bitterness of the people at the hands of the invaders, resulting in the growing insurgency—all of this was an open wound, and Al Qaeda, at the time headed in Iraq by Abu Musab al-Zarqawi, was the opportunistic infection rushing in. This is what I had suspected when I had met the group at the hospital today. Here was confirmation. I added this to the report I was typing up to send to my command: Al Qaeda is here.

"Their mission is not peace and understanding," said the Sheik. "These guys are what we call 'officially' ferocious. That is to say, they have license from the highest religious authorities to commit any sort of violence or mayhem they see fit. You Americans don't have to worry about them just yet. They have other priorities for the time being." And the Sheik looked at me in a no-nonsense way. "They are here to punish apostates—that is to say, the Shia—and to foment civil war." And he thought for a moment.

"It is convenient to place the blame for 9/11 entirely on Al Qaeda, and indeed they were deeply involved, but it is not quite that simple. I have many contacts in the Mukhabarat. I often eat breakfast with these men. They talk among themselves. Everyone in the Mukhabarat knows that the 9/11 attacks on your country were carried out by mercenaries. The actual men on those airplanes were hired, doing contract work for the Saudis. They were Baluch people. Like the Kurds, they are a stateless people with no country of their own, but they have a powerful ethnic identity, and Baluchistan, if you will, spreads across many borders—Iran, Pakistan, and Afghanistan. They are Sunni, they are ferociously devout, they have no fear of death, and they have a long tradition, going back centuries, of being mercenary fighters, quite willing to die for pay. The Saudis have made great use of their services, promising them that their families will be taken care of forever. They especially hire them for highly technical suicide missions." He paused. "Your enemy has many faces."

It would be a couple of more years before we'd see the famous picture of George W. Bush holding hands with Crown Prince Abdullah at the ranch in Texas. But already many were asking why the administration was so cozy and chummy with the Saudis after 9/11. Sitting there with the Sheik, I had a stronger conviction than ever that as far as retribution for 9/11 went, we had invaded the wrong country. That invading any country was the wrong way to "get" the perps who'd brought down the towers. Our enemies were a "stateless" coalition and some exceedingly strange bedfellows.

At any rate, Al Qaeda was now officially in Iraq. And I thought: *between Al Qaeda and the American-backed Shia death squads, civil war is just about a certainty.* Add to that the Iraqis' metastasizing resentment of the Americans, and we were headed toward full-on pandemonium.

The Sheik had plenty more to say about the new kids in town. He told me they came to Samarra from Mecca with trucks full of medical supplies—but that wasn't all. Each truck also carried a shipment of gold. The Sheik gave me official letters of transfer for the gold brought in by these men. Such a transfer was in keeping with the age-old tradition of Samarra being the "Gold City" of the Arab world, a veritable crossroads for the weighing, accounting, shipping, and trading of it. In the Sheik's paperwork, the gold's route was revealed as it traveled from city to city all over the world before arriving in Samarra: New York, Rome, London, Mecca, and Jeddah, to name just a few. I understood that I was glimpsing only a small part of the secret, borderless world of gold-trading and the associated subterranean world of unholy alliances. The group occupying the hospital building were, at that moment, in the early stages of establishing themselves, scoping out the city and the mood. Less than three years hence, they would famously destroy the Golden Mosque, a direct blow to the Shia population.

The Sheik had the papers showing those shipments of gold into the city, but he had even more for me that day, a truly tectonic scoop: he had papers showing that gold had also flowed out of the city, not long before the invasion, along with massive quantities of WMD—all under the auspices of the Mukhabarat. And where did the gold and the weapons go? Into Syria, he told me, to a giant weapons facility, one of the biggest in the world, a few miles south of Damascus.

"And what exactly went to that facility?" I asked.

"Everything," he said. "Everything sold to Saddam by the Americans. Sold to us and financed through your banks." He paused, lit another cigarette, and looked at me. "Sold to Saddam and actually paid for by you. What a world, eh?"

"But what kind of weapons?"

"Every known weapon of mass destruction, every killing agent made by man."

"Including . . . nuclear?"

"There are rumors, yes," he answered. "Of nuclear instrumentation. Detonators."

Detonators! This was major. Detonators meant plutonium. He never said "bombs," but he was quite emphatic about detonators.

"So it's all in Syria now," I said. "Why are you telling me this?"

"Because you must report this to your higher-ups, your people. They must not blow up that weapons depot. There are five different pits where the detonators might be. They must not use flame anywhere near any of them. It could cause multiple 'dirty bomb' explosions. It would be a catastrophe."

He was right, of course. I'd already written up my report to Maloney and Segura about the presence of Al Qaeda (which was, after all, one of the main reasons our intel unit had been sent here, to "get" Al Qaeda), the gold transfers, and the identity of the head guy. Now I added this vital addendum, with emphasis, about the weapons depot in Syria full of American WMD, including possible nuclear devices.

The response?

Zilch. Silence. No acknowledgment of any part of the report, not a murmur. Nothing.

But I did notice, in the immediate aftermath of my visit to the *madrassa*, a reduction in the sniping and mortar strikes in the area around the police station.

I thought perhaps I was seeing the fruits of diplomacy, that my work was not totally in vain.

My translator, meantime, quit his job, not even returning for his paycheck.

Soon after, somebody came into my office, carelessly sat on the antique rocking-camel, and splintered it.

CHAPTER 14

# ALL THAT GLITTERS

The MPs stomped through the house, barking threats and orders, ready to shoot anything that moved. I stayed calm and methodical. While the others ransacked Abu Seger's study, and his wife shrieked with fury, I thought: *No, not the study. This guy knew he was a target; he'd put it somewhere less obvious.* I went into the bedroom. As I did, I was thinking my hunch was right. Seger's wife, Sada (SAY-da), a stunningly attractive woman who was at least sixty, grew ever more frantic; I was obviously getting "warm."

Something else got my attention in the bedroom: a large, ornate photo album. As I approached the table where the album rested, Sada tried to physically restrain me. I had one of the MPs escort her from the room, telling him to take her outside but to be gentle about it. I told her I was sorry, and I was. I didn't enjoy inflicting this kind of pain at all.

I opened the album. Here was a human story the likes of which you don't often find in family albums: There were pictures of Abu Seger, Sada, their beautiful adult daughter, Saga (SAY-ja), and a certain unmistakable personage, Saddam Hussein; everyone was posing together with happy faces.

A couple of days earlier, the Sheik had come to the police station and rattled my cage.

"You'd better do this soon, or you'll lose him. He's getting ready to leave town. What are you waiting for? The second coming?"

He was getting impatient with our lack of action in apprehending Abu Seger, the man he'd told us about who was Saddam's banker, and I didn't blame him. I, too, was bewildered by the bureaucratic slowness I'd observed—unless, of course, there was any face-saving at stake, in which case they were a blur of speed. Abu Seger's house, as the Sheik had told us, was within a couple of blocks of the police station. Practically in our back yard.

We were finally cleared to pay an unannounced visit to Abu Seger. We may have been slow getting around to it, but when the night finally came, the MPs selected for the raid were pumped up on adrenaline and could hardly wait for the fun to begin. We hopped into our Humvees and were on our way.

The MPs kicked in the door and poured into the house, yelling threats and epithets. Abu Seger and his wife were taken totally by surprise. Seger—who, like the Sheik, looked entirely Western and was in his seventies, with a meek, mild affect—put up no resistance and was hustled out to a Humvee by the MPs while his wife shouted and implored. I felt bad for both of them, but we were there for a reason, to search the house for the huge stash of cash the Sheik told us we'd find.

That was when I found the photo album.

No wonder Sada didn't want us to see it. These pictures were a representation of an impossibly complex interrelationship between this family and Saddam, involving sex, vast quantities of money, and wicked political chess moves. I confiscated the album. But the album was not why we were here.

I approached an ornate armoire. As I did, Sada barged back into the room, having given the guards the slip, her voice rising in pitch and volume like a homing beacon. I opened the doors, and beheld the biggest stash of cash any of us had ever seen: three huge shrink-wrapped bundles of dollars, euros, and dinars. Behind me, Mrs. Seger moaned.

"Please! Please don't take it! This is all the money we have!"

"I'm sorry," I said. "I have to take it. I have no choice." She wailed like a mourner at a funeral as we loaded the cash onto dollies and moved it out of there. She was wailing for her husband, too, I have no doubt, but it was the sight of the money rolling out the door that made her voice rise to a keening pitch. As we were leaving, though, she thrust her husband's medications into my hands, and begged me to make sure he got them. I promised her I would.

It was midnight by the time we got Abu Seger and the cash back to the police station. A team got to work right away counting the money.

In the meantime, Abu Seger was in the interrogation room with Stavros, the Greek Arab-hater. I could hear shouting through the closed door. *I'd better get in there,* I thought, *before things get out of control.* Plus I wanted to get Seger's medications to him. My hand was on the doorknob when one of the office workers told me they had a tally of the seized cash: $40 million.

"Good," I said. "Enter that amount into the chain of evidence."

I pushed open the door just in time to hear Stavros screaming at Abu Seger about a recently discovered mass grave. When Seger tried to answer, Stavros bellowed "LIAR!" and bludgeoned him on the head with what looked like a rolled-up newspaper but with something hard concealed within. Abu Seger cried out in pain and crumpled to his knees.

I blocked Stavros from landing another blow, and seized the newspaper. Inside was a steel rod.

"Are you crazy?" I shouted. "We have possibly the highest source of information next to Saddam himself and you're trying to crack his skull? And for Christ's sake, this is an elderly man in poor health who's just been dragged out of his house! A little humanity, please!"

Stavros glared at me. His eyes burned with murder. He was in some kind of pumped-up state of righteous rage, but he backed off. May was in the room, too, cowering. She had a major crush on Stavros, and would, if not for a back injury, do anything Stavros might order her to do. They were a real pair of winners, those two. I got Seger up off his knees, sat him down, checked his vitals, and gave him his meds. He looked at me with pleading eyes. I knew I couldn't leave him alone with Stavros and May, or they'd kill him. I was reminded of myself at the mercy of my stepfather.

It was about 3 a.m. by that point. I hadn't slept for maybe twenty-four hours. I knew I needed to get some rest before I could come up with a rational strategy to get Seger out of there. I brought in a well-armed trooper, somebody I knew I could trust to follow my orders. I told him to stand guard over Abu Seger, that no one was to touch him or even speak to him, and that everyone, Stavros especially, was to leave him completely alone. Nearly nauseated with fatigue, I left to lie down in the airless little room that held my cot. My mind swarmed. *I've gone to war with the Psychopathic Keystone Cops,* I thought bitterly as I let myself sink into about a half hour of shallow sleep.

When I woke, I had a plan.

––––––––

Seger and I set out at dawn in a heavily armed convoy. I'd arranged for him to be transported, with me escorting him, to Tikrit, Saddam's home town, sixty-five miles north of Samarra, where other high-level prisoners were being kept. I warned everyone at the police station: Do NOT use ANY of our communications to talk about ANY of this. The word is surely out that Abu Seger is in our custody; hostile forces will either want to kill him or kidnap him because of what he might tell us. And they'll happily kill us, too. So for fuck's sake, keep this OFF the airwaves!

Seger and I were in the back seat on the long, jittery ride. I could clearly hear transmissions in Arabic coming from the hills to the west of the highway; I could also hear transmissions between the vehicles in our own convoy. *My God,* I thought; *if we can hear the enemy transmissions, they can hear ours, and track our every move. We're going to die.* Despite the tension, or perhaps because of it, Abu Seger talked freely as we sped along in the early-morning light. When I heard what he had to say, I doubly hoped we'd survive the trip and that the intelligence this man was giving would not be lost.

He spoke nonstop, as if relieved to be unburdening himself. He spilled it all; he gave the names of key bankers and other big players in major transactions involving weapons, gold, and cash. Plus he had all the details of the illicit exploitation of the UN "Oil for Food" program where billions of dollars from the sale of Iraqi oil, meant to compensate in part for the harsh sanctions imposed on Iraq by the United States after the Gulf War, were siphoned off through secret deals—enriching everyone from Saddam to Halliburton to major oil companies, while the common people suffered. He also named the banks through which major WMD purchases were made from the Americans and the British, the Bank of Iraq and the Bank of Credit and Commerce International

(BCCI). And he gave me a rare scoop: in some of these deals, there was little actual cash involved—instead, pressure plates used in the printing of American currency, along with related machinery and the special paper on which money is printed, plus the inks and dyes, were delivered by the BCCI so they could just manufacture all the cash they wanted.

I wrote it all down as fast as I could, intensely aware that Abu Seger was giving me this priceless intelligence precisely because I had stood up for him and protected him from crude bodily harm. I was also intensely aware that we could be vaporized at any moment as we sped along the highway, utterly exposed. I hadn't known the true meaning of the expression "the hills have eyes" until that interminable ride.

But we made it to Tikrit. Saddam had built palaces for himself all over Iraq, at least a hundred of them. The biggest and mightiest was in Baghdad, a veritable little city within a city, and all were obscenely lavish, but here in Tikrit, he unleashed and fine-tuned his fancy, as if he meant to create a different and distinct palace inspired by each of a thousand stories and legends, with himself as the mythical central figure. And considering that Saddam came up from being practically a barefoot beggar boy, the extravagant castles around his hometown made a particular "statement."

The VIP detainees were being held in one of the many custom-built palaces of Tikrit. This one was pink and utterly fantastical. Abu Seger gazed at it, shook his head, and laughed in an ironic sort of way.

"You're not going to believe this," he said. "History is playing tricks on me. This palace was designed by my daughter. And now I will be held prisoner inside it. It is like something out of an Arabian tale, is it not?"

Abu Seger's daughter! I recalled the photo I'd seen in the album I'd taken from Seger's bedroom. Of course! Saga, the beautiful daughter, was an architect and, famously, Saddam's mistress. I had known this, but it all came together at this moment. And I thought: *I should expect nothing less.* In the photos, everyone—Abu Seger, his wife, the daughter, and Saddam Hussein—were smiling. One could only imagine the complicated dynamics behind those smiles. When your unmarried daughter is having an affair with the dictator of your country, you not only don't object, but you cooperate and conspire. She, and you, are obliged to cultivate his pleasure. Perks and privileges served up with a spicy side dish of mortal danger.

We entered the palace. The interior was even more spectacular, with the walls and ceilings made of impossibly opulent pink quartz. I took one look at the thuggish American MPs on guard duty, and knew I couldn't leave Abu Seger alone with them any more than I could have left him alone with Stavros and May. I escorted him to a small octagonal turret room, also pink quartz, with cut-crystal windows and a built-in encircling quartz bench. The turret extended out into space from the main body of the palace, the Tigris flowing beneath.

For the next two hours, we talked in this unreal setting. He gave me more incalculably valuable intelligence, most of it pertaining to the perfidy and intertwined double-dealing of American big business and governmental and military leaders, going all the way back to 1959 and the recruitment of Saddam by the CIA, who put him and his Ba'ath party in power just a few years later. Seger gave names, dates, and details. Seger was plugged in for a long time with the major players in this recent invasion of Iraq, including Rumsfeld and Cheney, both of whom he knew personally, and had for many years. It was George H. W. Bush, Seger told me, who sold WMD to Saddam Hussein before the first Gulf War via the Carlyle Group. Seger could affirm this beyond any doubt, because, Seger said, he himself brokered the deal. Here was corroboration of what the colonel who'd shown me the WMD told me. With these revelations, Bush the Elder emerged as a major arch-villain.

A guard came in after a couple of hours to tell me that the return convoy to Samarra would be arriving soon. I shook hands with Seger, who looked at me and spoke matter-of-factly.

"You know, of course, that I won't be alive much longer," he said. "What I know, and what I have told you, is going to get me killed. Either by my own people or yours."

I marveled at the calm courage of this elderly man, with his soft, manicured banker's hands, hands that had probably never wielded anything more lethal than a letter opener.

Before I left, I told the guards in my best voice of authority: Keep this man safe, at all costs. Do *not* let any harm come to him. Do not let *anyone* near him.

And I left Abu Seger sitting in the beautiful pink quartz turret room. I went outside. Between the long night, the staggering amount of information Seger gave me, and the utter surrealism of the setting, I was a little dazed. I walked down Saddam Hussein Boulevard. Tikrit is a smallish city, and it hugs the length of a major deep, wide bend of the Tigris River. It has many ancient, fascinating ruins. Though parts of Tikrit are dry and dusty like so many cityscapes in Iraq, all is lush and green and dotted with date palms where the river meanders through it.

I knew the pink palace was not the only extravagant fantasy castle in town. I soon found another one, surely also designed by Saga, made entirely of rare black Spanish marble (all that Spain could produce in a year, I would later learn). It, too, was wide open, not a soul in sight. I went in. Apparently the looters had not yet hit this place. There was a thirty-foot-long hardwood table, and lo and behold: the lavish gold-trimmed white chair, more like a throne, in which Saddam Hussein sat and posed for the world-famous photograph we've all seen. I couldn't resist, and I doubt anyone else would have been able to, either. I plopped myself into the chair.

From this vantage, I contemplated the Saddam's-eye view: to the right was a wall of tall windows. They faced toward Kurdistan, Syria, Mosul. Exploring further, I noted the many small adjoining rooms off the main hall: each contained a bed made of fancy hardwood inlaid with mother-of-pearl. No desks, no chairs, no office equipment. Just beds. It was obvious what these rooms were for. All of this grotesquely self-indulgent *Arabian Nights* splendor had a particular resonance, fresh as I was from Abu Seger's revelations about where so much of the oil-for-food money went.

Thinking of Abu Seger, I got a strong feeling I should go back to the pink palace and check on him. My instinct was right; I was furious to find that not only had they moved Abu Seger to another room, but he now had company. He and a huge scary-looking Iraqi sat together on a Persian prayer rug. Seger and the scary guy were plainly acquainted. Seger introduced me, and I recognized the name. This man was one of Saddam Hussein's international assassins, and he and Seger knew one another from when both were in the Mukhabarat.

Though the man seemed to be deferential toward Abu Seger, and protective of him, I was instantly wary. Anyone still loyal to Saddam might very well kill Abu Seger for his betrayal. This fellow looked as though he could snap Seger's neck with one hand in a single unguarded moment. I separated them, moving Abu Seger to a room far away from the assassin guy and assigning a guard for him. I explained to Abu Seger why I had done this. He merely shrugged philosophically, as if he didn't think his life was worth much at this point anyway.

The two of us had a farewell conversation. Seger made it clear that he was not overly impressed with the methods and discipline of the Americans as compared to the iron-fisted ways of the Mukhabarat. I had to agree. His personal regard for me, though, was another matter: He pulled a silver ring set with a blue stone from his finger and held it out.

"Remember me," he said.

I wear that ring to this day.

I left for Samarra. The next time I was to see Abu Seger, it would be in a very different place.

# CHAPTER 15

# SOMETHING WICKED

The smell of Gauloises smoke, an aroma that could surely raise the dead, woke me from deep, sodden sleep. The Sheik sat comfortably, watching me. I could tell he'd been there for a while. Lighting one of his cigarettes was his polite way of rousing me without having to shake me by the shoulder.

I was back at the police station after my long, long day and night. I'd entered into the chain of evidence the extensive detailed and invaluable information given by Abu Seger. Everything we got from him—cash, banking statements, and the reports I wrote up—went through the CHIMS (Combined Human Intelligence Management) system via Segura, Maloney, and Pappas. After entering the latest intel, I had put my head down and dropped instantly into dreamless oblivion.

"Congratulations on catching Abu Seger," said the Sheik.

"Thank you for telling us about him." I sat up blearily.

"How much money did you find in his house?"

"Forty million."

The Sheik just laughed.

"Oh, no, no, no." He showed me some banking papers. "Did you look under the floor?"

A return visit to Abu Seger's house and a thorough ripping-up of the floorboards yielded another $710 million, for a total of $750 million. The additional mountain of cash was seized and also entered into the already bulging chain of evidence. Meanwhile, though I was waiting for some sort of word from Tikrit about Abu Seger, I heard nothing, and soon learned why: because the CIA had swept in and taken him to Abu Ghraib.

Very quickly on the heels of the cash being counted, turned in, and entered into the chain of evidence, Maloney and Segura showed up in Samarra, giving me cagey looks. I would eventually learn that I was legally entitled to 20 percent of that seized money, though I certainly had not known it when we raided Abu Seger's house.

Most of us have never heard of the False Claims Act, also known as the Lincoln Law, originally passed in 1863 in response to rampant fraud on the part of private contractors, who sold broken-down horses, rancid food, rusty defective weapons, and such to the Union Army during the Civil War. Gosh, what a surprise, huh? Under the new law, a private citizen could "blow the whistle" and be entitled to a percentage of money or value recovered. The law is still in effect today, was beefed up in 1986 during Reagan's massive military buildup and the resultant feeding frenzy of fraud on the part of private contractors. The idea, both back in 1863 and today, is to offer an incentive, a healthy "finder's fee" to the citizen whose actions recover spuriously obtained treasure for the government. The mountain of shrink-wrapped money in Abu Seger's house could only have got there via fraud and was found only because of the intel given to me by the Sheik.

No, I had no idea I was entitled to a percentage, but Maloney and Segura very likely knew. What I did know was that the $750 million was whisked away and never mentioned again. Later, they would deny it ever existed.

———

The Sheik was a priceless asset. Everything he gave us about Abu Seger turned out to be impeccable, his credibility so far almost 100 percent. The Sheik was responsible for the welfare of the people in his province, and was aware of absolutely everything that went on there. He knew names, places, dates, and minute details, because people came and told him. A herd of goats couldn't cross the highway, I was sure, without the Sheik knowing about it. When he came bearing any information at all, I gave him my full attention. Especially when that information pertained directly to the lives and safety of American troops.

The Sheik had told me that his father cooperated with the British a couple of generations before, and had had high regard for their competence, efficiency, cohesion, discipline, integrity, and so forth. The Sheik, knowing that the Brits and the Americans were close allies, shared a language, and had always worked in accord, assumed that the Americans would be the same as the Brits. By now, I'm sorry to say, I knew that this was credit the Americans did not deserve. Nevertheless, the information brought to me by the Sheik—plans for mortar attacks, ambushes, and such—could save American lives. If, of course, the command took heed.

The Sheik appeared at the station one day and told me of plans by certain factions to pack culverts beneath roadways with explosives (looted from Al Qa'qaa), the infamous IEDs (Improvised Explosive Devices) that would maim and kill so many Americans and other coalition troops. At this point, this crude but highly effective mode of guerilla warfare was not well-known, and the acronym had not entered the popular consciousness as it soon would.

I duly reported the Sheik's warning to Balad. Their reaction? Silence. I later found out that they laughed and tossed the report aside.

On another day, the Sheik came and told me of a plot afoot to kill a group of soldiers who took after-duty swims in an irrigation pond close to a nearby town. He said the plan was to re-wire the electric pump serving that particular pond so that the swimming soldiers would be electrocuted. I sent a "flash" report, the equivalent of a Mayday, to headquarters: Stop what you're doing and get on this right away. Lives are in imminent danger!

The response from headquarters? Again, nothing. Silence.

I'd like to stress something here: the usual, reasonable response to an intel report by an agent to his command is an acknowledgment from the command in the form of an IIR (Individual Intelligence Report) or CIR (Counterintelligence Individual Report). It's a confirmation that the message was received, paid attention to, and considered, and asks any questions that might be raised. Starting with the discovery of the WMD in Balad, never, ever did I get an IIR or a CIR from my command in response to any of my intel reports, whether a report concerned plans to plant IEDs, to electrocute swimming soldiers, the presence of Al Qaeda just down the street, the transport of nuclear material across borders, or where bin Laden might be found. No questions, no comments, no interest, no curiosity. It was as if they decided, from the moment I reported the stash of WMD in the bunker and they suppressed the find, that any response from them would be affirmation of the work I was doing, making it harder for them to discredit me later. And in the case of WMD or actually capturing bin Laden, there were those higher than my command who, it seemed, would do anything to kill and bury that intel.

———————

Soon after, I had occasion to go down to Balad. I went to intel headquarters. I found the "experts" sitting in their air-conditioned room at their computers, checking their e-mail and watching DVD movies. I confronted a certain Sgt. White (not his real name), known as the "Svengali" of intelligence reports. This was a guy known to be a stickler for rules and detail. I asked him about the "flash" report I'd sent. He looked at me with a bland, complacent face.

"We didn't act on it because it wasn't correctly formatted. Capital letters were not properly used, and you failed to include the requisite two periods separating sentences."

I gaped. I was dumbfounded. Was I hearing him wrong? Were my ears plugged up? Had I wandered into some Kafka-type tale about the distorted banal absurdity of bureaucracy?

And I thought: *No wonder the American military can't win a war.*

I had already experienced plenty of this baffling nonaction on the part of my "superiors," but this was something of an epiphany: nothing ever happened when a report was submitted until and unless some sort of credit for personal/ political advancement on the part of those in charge could be mined from that report. The fact that the Sheik's intel had so far been pure gold was of barely secondary importance to these complacent paper-pushers. Their real agenda stood exposed.

Then the Sheik brought up a serious and slightly awkward bit of business. He said he needed to be able to pay the various people he'd recruited in the effort to bring intel to us. I totally agreed, and thought this a perfectly reasonable request. And I trusted the Sheik completely to be my "truth" filter; he wouldn't come to me with anything he didn't know to be twenty-four-karat genuine. I also knew he wasn't talking about vast quantities of money—twenty, thirty, fifty, or a hundred dollars would go a long, long way in compensating people who were risking their lives coming forward with vital information.

I took another trip to Balad to put in a request that money be withdrawn from the Intelligence Asset Fund, a circulating, refreshed fund of fifty thousand dollars for exactly this purpose. The commander in charge was one Major Gerald Hawkins (not his real name) another brave warrior who rarely left the air-conditioned safety zone of the headquarters.

I made my request to Hawkins emphatically, stressing that these valuable sources would dry up if people were not compensated, not to mention that it would be very bad for our already deteriorating image if we didn't give something in return.

I was met with a look as if I'd just asked for the keys to Fort Knox.

"We don't have any money," said Hawkins. "Tell you what, though—here's a five-gallon can. Fill it with gas and give 'em that."

I ended up paying people out of my own pocket.

Later, I'd learn that Major Hawkins put himself in for two Bronze Stars—the award for "heroic or meritorious achievement or service."

———

A call from Abu Ghraib from someone at the transportation department not long after my return from Tikrit and my short trip to Balad gave me an instant bad, sinking feeling:

"Remember that older guy you took to Tikrit from Samarra? He's here now. You'd better come down."

I'd promised Abu Seger that no harm would come to him, that he'd be protected. I recalled his words, spoken with calm resignation: "I won't be alive much longer."

I was queasy with apprehension during the two-and-a-half hour ride, my gizzard in my mouth every mile of the way. As usual, the highway between Samarra and Baghdad was almost empty. The scenery looked even more monochromatic and flat than usual. Mile after mile of desert stretching all the way to Saudi Arabia, Syria and Jordan in the west and to Iran in the east seemed a perfect reflection of my bleak, empty, and wretched state of mind.

I rode with several transport guys in a plain van, not a Humvee or other military-type vehicle, figuring a civilian vehicle would be less likely to draw fire when we'd have to make that westward turn onto Death Alley. My dread of what I would find when I got to Abu Ghraib overshadowed my fear of getting shot at or blown up.

At the prison, the transport guy who'd summoned me showed me along a maze of hallways. Many eyes were on me as I passed and we got closer to the infirmary and Building 1-A. In one section, they were carrying out "punishment" of unruly prisoners. I saw Iraqis strapped to "quiet chairs;" some of them looked as if they'd been there for more than a day. The looks on the faces of personnel were both guilty and accusing. Like: Who the hell are you, and do I have to worry about you reporting on what you're seeing? Luckily for them, I barely noticed, so intent was I on seeing Abu Seger.

And then, there he was, on a gurney in a hallway between the infirmary and Building 1-A, alone. Oh, he was being watched, all right, but there was no one administering to him. All they cared about was who might get access to him. As a medic, I was allowed to approach. *Too late,* I thought when I was a couple of feet away. *He's dead.*

But I was astonished to find him still alive. When I had a closer look, though, I wished for his sake that he were not.

He was beyond comatose. I immediately saw a type of head injury known as "contrecoup," where the brain is damaged twice from one blow: there's the injury at the site of impact, and then the brain is injured again on the direct opposite side due to being displaced and slammed against the inside of the skull by the force of the blow. One of Abu Seger's eyes was bulging and the socket dark and bruised, typical of contrecoup. He was still breathing, but had gone into what's known as "Cheyne-Stokes" respiration, distinctive and typical of terminal head trauma: many rapid breaths followed by a long, agonizing pause of no breathing at all, then more rapid breaths, then another long pause. It's a horrible thing to watch, making it seem over and over as if the sufferer has finally been released by death, but then the breathing starts up again. It can go on for hours. Another name for this is the "death rattle." The sheer blind life-force in the all-but-dead body is profoundly disturbing.

I looked at the transport guy who'd accompanied me, and spoke a single word: "Agency?"

The man nodded.

It was as Abu Seger himself had predicted: *What I have told you is going to get me killed. Either by my own people or yours.* Of course, he couldn't be allowed to live after revealing how much he knew about the deeply hidden double-dealing with Iraq of Reagan and both Bushes, but most especially, Bush the Elder.

There was nothing at all to be done. If I'd been a priest, I'd have given Abu Seger his Last Rites. As it was, I touched his shoulder and told him farewell, and that I was sorry, so sorry. I turned and left for Samarra with a sick and heavy heart, ill and shaken with a terrible, overwhelming sense of having betrayed him. I would, I knew, live the rest of my life with the image of the dying old man on the bloody gurney in the lonely prison hallway, his head pulped. And I also knew: *We've betrayed this entire country.*

Much later, and a world away, I would learn that not long after my sad trip to Abu Ghraib, an American sedan pulled up to the field hospital in Balad. A tall Anglo in civilian clothes, baseball cap on his head, got out, opened the trunk, and dumped the badly-beaten corpse of an elderly man onto the pavement.

# CHAPTER 16

# THE BELIEVER

The scene in the interrogation room when I opened the door might have been conceived by the Marquis de Sade: my 6'6" colleague, Jason Richter, had a blindfolded man on the floor, face down, hands tied behind him. Richter's huge foot was between the prisoner's shoulder blades, and he was pulling both the man's arms straight up at a hideous angle. Another man, an associate from a different unit, sat on a sofa, calmly watching the spectacle like a Roman in the Colosseum, and a third man, a translator, hovered. My first step into the room was accompanied by the dreadful *crack* of the prisoner's shoulders popping out of their sockets, followed by a scream of animal agony.

"Whoa, whoa, Jason, what are you doing?" I yelled. Richter worked under me, and so far, I'd given him the benefit of the doubt, assuming he was conducting interrogations ethically. I'd never seen him indulge in cruelty before. In the space of a second, I understood the extent of my error. Prisoner abuse had become a virulently spreading contagion. And Richter was a charter member of the Mahmoud fan club.

I managed to get the hulking Richter off the detainee, who by now had fainted. Seizing the opportunity to take remedial action while the man was unconscious, I pressed the shoulders in, rotated the arms down and popped the shoulder joints back into their sockets. I could feel the instantaneous release of tension in the man's body as I did this. The prisoner came to. I took the blindfold off him and gave him some water. The man looked at all four of us in turn without any fear. His gaze was steady and focused as he sized each of us up. Richter and the associate just stared dumbly.

A few minutes earlier, someone had asked me if any intel had been extracted from the guy knocked out by a mortar, who'd come to and had been taken for questioning by Richter.

"What are you talking about?" I said. "What guy? I don't know anything about any of this," and had gone into the interrogation room.

Now, getting a good look at the captive, I saw much that was not usual: he had no moustache, just about unheard of in Iraq. His hair was reddish, and in different clothing, he could pass for Western on any street in the USA. His body was superbly fit; he had obviously been training rigorously. He wore a black headband with Arabic writing on it, in gold.

I got the details of his capture: he'd appeared during a skirmish in an open area near the Golden Mosque, had walked onto the scene of the conflict speaking into a radio, apparently calling mortar fire onto an Abrams tank, was knocked out by the percussion of a mortar meant to hit the tank but which fell short. And so he was arrested and brought in the Abrams to the police station.

I had the translator tell the prisoner that I was impressed with his courage and fortitude, and also had the translator say that I regretted the brutish treatment, that this was not the way interrogations should be handled.

As the translator spoke my words, I could see the prisoner's dignity and pride reassert themselves and the life flow back into him. I knew that an interrogator is far more likely to get true, valuable, useful information via decent humane treatment, as with Abu Seger, than through threats, beatings, and torture. And indeed, the man was forthcoming.

He told me he came from Syria to Samarra to be "with the Caliph."

"And last night," he said, "I succeeded: I spent the entire night with the Caliph!"

He said it again and again, plainly in awe, as someone would be who believed he was participating in the fulfillment of holy prophecy. Though I didn't know who or what he meant, I sensed powerful conviction behind the words. And I quickly put it together that this was no ordinary prisoner. The translator identified, reluctantly and with palpable fear, like his predecessor's, the man's distinctive headband: he was Al Qaeda, like the people occupying the hospital.

I could not have known it at the time, but I was at the confluence of history. The shoulders I'd just popped back into place were those of Muhammad al Adnani, the man who would eventually become second in command of Al Qaeda's later, more extreme mutation: ISIS, led by Abu Bakr al-Baghdadi, the guy we'd questioned on night one in Samarra. Nor could I have known at the time that the mysterious "Caliph" mentioned by the prisoner was none other than al-Baghdadi. Again, I was impressed, in the person of this man, by the focus, training, courage, true belief, and powerful discipline of the "enemy," qualities depressingly lacking in everyone around me, from the enlisted to the officers to the distant top command pulling the strings from far, far away.

The contrast was stark and telling. By comparison, we were a disjointed army of frivolous, greedy, ignorant, incompetent sadists from the other side of the planet who had no idea of who or what we were up against. The only place where a corresponding intensity and purity of purpose existed on our side, I reflected, was in the soundproof boardrooms of the unholy military-industrial alliance Eisenhower had warned us about. That was our "Caliphate."

Still sick with the memory of Abu Seger betrayed, savaged, and dying at Abu Ghraib, I was sick also with a deepening sense of foreboding beyond that personal catastrophe. The encounter with the prisoner with the focused intensity and the black Al Qaeda headband; the fury of the tribal warlord after the wedding massacre; the myopic double-dealing of my command in the wake of the discovery of the WMD and their casual dismissiveness toward life-and-death warnings from the Sheik; the steady escalation of thuggery and sadism on the part of my countrymen and the refusal of the command to act on it or even acknowledge my strenuous reporting of it; promises large and small horribly broken; vast quantities of cash and treasure vanished; and a sense of duplicitous powerful forces and entities working behind the scenes and lying to the world—all of it put me in mind of an ominous old saying:

Sow the wind, reap the whirlwind.

## CHAPTER 17

# HEART OF DARKNESS

The abrupt cessation of screaming made me sit up in alarm. I jumped out of my chair, went round to the interrogation room and yanked open the door. May hurried out, pink and disheveled, avoiding my eyes, nearly colliding with me. Stavros sat in a chair, tilted back casually, cigarette dangling from his mouth, pistol in his hand. He squinted at me through the smoke curling up into his eyes, smirked, then chambered a round with a smug *clack-clack*. He had a look about him of a man who'd just finished a strenuous but deeply satisfying task.

Picture the layout: a windowless room about three and a half feet wide and about eight feet long, a prisoner lying in a heap next to the filthy toilet at the far end of the room.

The prisoner, a barely-grown boy, had been brought to the police station in Samarra by the MPs that evening not long after my trip to Abu Ghraib and taken into the interrogation room to be "questioned" by Stavros. I'm sorry to say that by then, we were all way too accustomed to the shouts, the muffled screams, and the *thud* of bodies being slammed into the wall. What I was not accustomed to was the sudden silence.

I brushed past Stavros, checked the kid, who looked even younger lying there helpless, and found he was unconscious but breathing. The gun in Stavros' hand gave me a pretty good idea of one of the "techniques" he'd employed. It was called "artificial execution," and was strictly illegal. You put a loaded gun to the prisoner's head, tell him he has one minute to live, that you'll kill him and every member of his family unless he talks. When the prisoner just cries and screams in gibbering terror, you beat him into unconsciousness. Stavros was a fulfilled man, in his element.

The kid's color was okay, and I couldn't see any serious wounds on him. I figured he'd live. I signaled the MPs to get him out of there. They came in, grabbed him roughly, and dragged him down the hall to the holding pen.

Here's where I confess I was partly responsible for what happened next. We all staggered off to sleep late that night. My conscience was heavy, but I was exhausted, and, I realized, becoming inured to Stavros' chronic violence. This can happen. You grow psychic calluses, mostly out of self-protection. It's not at all what you intend, but it happens.

We woke early the next morning to cloying, smothering heat. When it's hot like that first thing, you know it's going to get bad, that tempers will be short and mercy in short supply. The MPs were already bringing in prisoners. The atmosphere was charged, dangerous. There was an attitude in the air: no more fucking around—you're going to talk and what happens to you doesn't matter. Stavros looked refreshed and ready for action. He was well aware I'd complained before about rough treatment of prisoners, and he was looking sideways at me on this morning, as if to say: You gonna tell about the kid yesterday, or not?

I didn't say anything. I should have, but I didn't, and Stavros, emboldened by my nonaction, seemed to puff up a little.

Then came a rocket attack, aimed at the police station, and probably the interrogation room specifically. It missed, but a huge *thud* shook the building while we all dived for cover. Somebody had been seen running away in the wake of the attack. The MPs knew what house he'd run to, and were hot to raid.

I went along. We approached the house, a few blocks away, forced our way in, found nobody home, but did find an AK-47 under a couch. We walked through the rooms, weapons at the ready, when we heard a calm, pleasant voice behind us.

"Greetings, my friends!"

I swung around. A man in clerical garb stood just inside the front door, smiling. He held both hands up, not exactly in "surrender" mode, more like: I'm harmless, let's all just be reasonable. This is, of course, how many a suicide bomber sidles up to his victims, a smile on his face and explosives under his robes. The guys with me kept their weapons on him, shouted at him to keep his hands where they were, to not move a goddamned inch. I was jumpy, too, but the man and I looked at each other. The communication was as nonverbal and pure as my moment out in the desert with the wolf. I thought: *This is an actual holy man.* Crazy, I know, but my fear dissolved. Whatever the word "holy" might mean, this guy was real. I spoke to him, explained why we were there, and why there was enough tension in that room to split an atom.

Calm and friendly, he listened and said he understood perfectly. He said that in all situations, it's possible to do better than we are doing, that he had seen us come into this house and so he was here to be of any assistance he could. He was serene and completely unafraid. I decided that he could not possibly be carrying a bomb or weapon without giving off some sort of involuntary signal—sweat, eye movements, or a vocal quaver, however small.

He and I regarded one another for a few more seconds, transcending, so it felt to me, such minor considerations as nationality and ideology, and then he turned and left. The house, it turned out, was empty.

We went back to the station. Another teenager, suspected of knowing something about the rocket attack, had been brought in by the MPs and was in Stavros's clutches. This kid was familiar—he was the same one I'd noticed the day before walking back and forth in the street, possibly counting off paces, measuring the distance between the station and wherever the rocket had been fired from. Now he was on the verge of hysteria, screaming and blubbering. Stavros, feeding off the kid's terror, was growing enraged. Pressure was building. Stavros had him out front and was bellowing into the kid's face:

"We're gonna kill you!" *He means it,* I thought. *He really is going to kill this kid.* It was likely that the boy did know something about the attack, but I could see that there was no way, short of full-on torture, that we were going to get that info out of him. I couldn't let that happen. Fresh from my encounter with the "Holy Man," and regretting my nonaction with the kid Stavros had beaten up the night before, I knew I had to intervene. I got between the kid and Stavros.

"It's not worth it," I said to Stavros, whose face twitched and twisted as if he had some kind of palsy. "We have to let him go." I was doing my best to channel the calm, sure demeanor of the Holy Man. I didn't think I was doing such a great job of it, because I could hear my own raised voice and knew my face was hardly serene, but somehow I got through to Stavros. He looked at me for a few seconds, teeth bared, then shoved the kid away as he let go of him. The boy was gone like a jackrabbit.

I may have bought that particular kid a reprieve, but others would pay for it. Now Stavros was thoroughly pissed. He disappeared inside, and soon he and May were back in the little room with another fifteen-year-old prisoner.

Within twenty minutes, Stavros was done with this one. He slammed open the door and yelled:

"Get this piece of shit out of here!" Now I could smell burning flesh. Appalled, I went in, May slipping guiltily away in the confusion. Like his predecessor, the kid lay in an unconscious heap in the corner, but with an extra touch—a burning cigarette stuck in each ear.

"I'm taking responsibility for this prisoner right now," I shouted to anyone who might be listening. The interpreter, who'd been in there with Stavros, May and the prisoner, was still hovering around, wringing his hands and muttering in Arabic. "Stavros did this to him, right?" I demanded of the interpreter. Reluctantly, obviously fearing us and the entire ghastly situation, he said yes.

I did my best to fix up the prisoner, yanking out the cigarettes, putting salve in his burnt ears, testing his reflexes, and making sure he was breathing okay, then got him out of there. If he regained consciousness, it was after he'd been taken to the holding area. I barely had time to get that one out of the room before Stavros was back in there with yet another.

This one, too, was unconscious but breathing after twenty minutes. He was leaning against the wall, limbs splayed, head hanging on his chest.

"The piece of shit is faking it," said one of the MPs, reaching down, covering the prisoner's mouth and pinching his nose with one big hand. The boy didn't respond at all. I was watching someone being murdered right there in front of me.

"Cut that out, for Christ's sake!" I said, knocking the MP's hand away. He did stop, but with great reluctance. I was interfering with his fun.

I ventilated the prisoner with a mask and an air bag. He rolled his head and groaned, though he didn't quite regain consciousness. What to do with him? He was half dead. There was no hospital I could send him to. All I could do was send him back to the holding area, where he would live or die on the concrete floor with the others.

It was like an assembly line. Stavros was on a rampage. Soon he was back in the room with a fourth prisoner. This time, when he flung open the door, I saw right away that something was different. The boy on the floor wasn't merely not breathing, he was turning blue. *Cardiac arrest*, I thought instantly. I rushed in and put a stethoscope to his chest. I was right: No heartbeat. This kid was all of maybe fifteen years old. There had been relatively little screaming this time. What had Stavros done? Knelt on his chest? Delivered a blow to the sternum?

The MPs just kind of stood there watching while I worked, their eyes gleaming. They wanted this kid to die. They were hungry for it, like hyenas smelling raw meat.

I started CPR immediately. For the first two or three minutes, I might as well have been working on a corpse. He was limp, blue, and totally unresponsive. I kept on: I thumped him and ventilated him, watching for the return of color, not wanting to stop long enough to listen for a heartbeat. He finally gasped and took a breath, his color returning. I listened and heard his heart pounding. He was alive. Like the others, there was nowhere to send him but the holding area.

I took Stavros aside. I was sweating and shaking with fury and exertion. These kids, beaten to the edge of death, were awakening all my old trauma with my rotten stepfather.

"I can't take anymore," I told him. "You can't do this. You're going to end up killing us all! Don't you get it? We're surrounded, outgunned. They hate us more every day because of this crap!"

"So what?" he snarled, his face churning. "Do I give a shit?"

"We could be killed. We could be charged with war crimes, you bloody fool!"

"I don't give a shit about that, either," he said, though I saw something shift behind his eyes. Frenzied with blood lust though he was at that moment, he still had a streak of self-preservation operating in his crazed head. He glared venomous hatred at me. No doubt he was imagining sticking lit cigarettes in my ears and beating me until I stopped breathing. He turned and walked away. Perhaps to find May and have a little post-torture coitus. The day's work was over. It was barely noon.

God only knew what kind of sick erotic games my "colleagues" May and Stavros played behind the closed door to the torture room. She was always in there with him when he was "at work." Her well-established shtick the rest of the time was to sow a swath of sexual tension wherever she went; she was a tease in the worst sense of the word. She was especially good at bringing out the big dumb battling ape in the guys around her, setting them against each other and getting them all worked up into a sort of primate competition. It would have been funny if it weren't so dangerous and pathetic.

May had already proven her prowess as a tease back in the camp in Kuwait. In Samarra, which was becoming a genuine combat zone, way more dangerous than Kuwait or Balad, I'd see her doing her giggly, flirty little baby-doll act amidst simple-minded brutes, and next thing I knew they'd be giving me malevolent looks, probably with May's breathy little voice still tickling their ears. Certainly they were not giving their full attention to the increasingly volatile situation around us as our popularity with the locals plummeted. Christ knows what she said, or promised, or actually did, but like Stavros, she was trouble wherever she went.

She worshiped Stavros, though, and would do anything he told her to do. He wore the pants in that little romance. There was no doubt he was a sick puppy who derived special pleasure from inflicting pain; it's not hard to imagine one carnal impulse feeding the other while May pleasured him, or herself, or both, all of it in front of, or possibly including, the terrified prisoner. Later, when we would learn of similar crude psycho-sexual torment inflicted at Abu Ghraib in combination with physical torture, I realized that we in Samarra had had a prescient little glimpse, thanks to two of our own.

And Mahmoud slithered across the back of my mind. I thought of what one of my first assets in Samarra, the Egyptian lawyer who'd worked for Halliburton, had told me about the torture experiments in Saudi Arabia during the first

Gulf War and the use of specific sexual humiliations on Arab prisoners. Mahmoud, Mukhabarat alumnus that he was, would know all about that. I could picture him cannily sizing up Stavros and May and their natural talents, pegging them as perfect candidates to carry out this sort of exotic abuse, then suggesting it to them in such a way that they would think it was their own idea. I had an image of Mahmoud as a king cobra, rising and swaying hypnotically.

I wrote up and submitted full, detailed medical reports on all of that day's youthful detainees, as I always did, and included the truth about who inflicted these near-fatal injuries and how. I included a demand that my reports of torture be forwarded to Gen. Janis Karpinski, commander of the 800th Military Police Brigade, the force responsible for the operation of at least a dozen coalition-run detention facilities in Iraq, including Abu Ghraib and our mini-detention facility in Samarra. I had no other way to get to Karpinski except through my chain of command, which meant I had no choice but to rely on Maloney and Pappas to deliver the message of their own criminal negligence. I didn't have a great deal of confidence that this would happen, but I wanted it on the record.

And of course, I made copies of those reports, as I always did.

I needed solutions, and I needed them fast. Maybe there was a "lost in translation" problem. Maybe a different interpreter would use words less likely to enrage Stavros. A desperate measure, I knew, but I had to do something. It happened that a personnel carrier pulled up in front of the police station soon after that terrible day of reviving the dead and my desperate exchange with Stavros. The back opened, the ramp came down, and a couple of already-beat-to shit prisoners were revealed huddling in the vehicle. It was quite a scene; other prisoners, hoods over their heads, were tied up and waiting beneath the stairs for their "turn." People were running in and out of the police station. Officers from the liaison unit who'd arrived with the personnel carrier were milling about. Local people stood and watched the show.

I went outside and approached one of those officers. He was not someone I was acquainted with. I do remember that he was a captain, was Japanese-American, and had a look of sense and authority about him, as if maybe I could have a reasonable conversation with him.

I approached, and in a low, discreet voice explained the situation. "We may be having trouble because of translation problems," I said, "and you'd be doing us a great favor if you could loan us one of your translators."

There was a pensive moment when it seemed that he was considering my words. *Thank God*, I said to myself, *there's somebody around here with some sense.*

He looked at me, turned and looked toward other officers in his group who were in the midst of dragging the prisoners out of the personnel carrier, looked at the dozens of people here, there, and everywhere around us, some just watching, others going in and out of the police station, and then turned back to me and exploded.

"*God damn it!*" he yelled, his voice loud enough to be heard a block away. "There's no way I'm gonna give you *my assets* so that *you* can commit *espionage* on this site!"

Shocked, I cringed. *Espionage?* If ever there was a dangerously loaded word whose meaning is scarcely guaranteed to be agreed upon by any two different people hearing it, it's "espionage." For sure, it's not a word to be tossed around carelessly, let alone shouted at the top of one's lungs in a crowd, unless your possible intent is to accuse, put on trial, and execute in one stroke. It's a word with dire connotations. Throughout history, to be merely accused of "espionage," with its associated whiff of treachery, was to quite possibly be pushed off a cliff, knifed, or discretely garroted on a dark night.

People were turning and looking at the officer and at me. They'd heard the word, loud and clear. Anyone hearing it could interpret it to suit his or her bias, attitude, grudge, or point of view, never mind truth, accuracy, or nuance. To Iraqi ears, it could suggest that I was the "enemy;" to American ears, it would suggest that I was treasonous against the Stars and Stripes. It was absurd either way, but I felt a real wave of danger rush over me.

And in that moment, I understood what this particular man meant when he shouted that potent and dangerous word. He meant that what I was doing—reporting on the violations and atrocities being committed by my colleagues—was "espionage." Plainly, he'd heard about me and my reports, and sided solidly with Maloney and Segura that I was interfering with the "mission," was a turncoat. I wilted under this insane tirade. He could have been marking me with a death sentence then and there.

Of course, it was true that I was, in a sense, engaged in "espionage." I was an intelligence agent, and that's what intelligence agents do. My mistake was to strive to keep everybody alive.

I had many moments of epiphany in Iraq, and this was a major one. None of these people, I thought, has the remotest idea of what they are doing or why. It's a free-for-all, a farce, a deadly and mirthless comedy of errors.

"Never mind," I said in an even voice, and walked away.

---

I was acutely aware of the growing restlessness in the city. The frequency of mortar attacks had increased once more, occurring now almost nightly. We were behaving like lunatics. The dissension within our own ranks was on display like street theatre.

And in fact, the Sheik came to me with a warning. This time, the twinkle was absent from his eye.

"People are bitter and enraged. There will be a major attack on you Americans in approximately two weeks."

When the Sheik spoke, I listened. And other locals, including my latest translator, corroborated the Sheik's message:

"We like you and trust you, Agent Ford. We regard you as a brother, and so we are telling you of what's going to happen," he told me in secret.

I warned Maloney.

"You have to put a stop to the abuse and sadism. Get these amateurs out of here. Things are about to get deadly."

Maloney reacted with mockery, the first refuge of a scoundrel.

"Oh? And when, in your seasoned, expert opinion, Sgt. Ford, will we be having this big problem?" he sneered

"Well, Lt. Col. Maloney," I said, "in just about two weeks, we're gonna lose the whole thing. They'll give us such a fight, they'll drive us right out of Iraq."

Maloney gave me a look as if I were raving. The warning was ignored. The abuse not only didn't stop, it got worse, starting the very next day. Stavros in particular seemed to be nourished by the crude burgeoning cruelty. He was getting in touch, so to speak, with his inner sadist.

I was at the end.

With the Sheik's words and the bellowing of the Japanese-American captain sounding in my ears, I put in for a transfer. I knew I'd have to wait where I was while the bureaucratic gears did their slow grind, and that I might not survive these last days in Samarra, but if I did, I could maybe be out of there in one piece by the time the Sheik's prophecy came true.

# CHAPTER 18

# OZYMANDIUS

I know where Saddam Hussein is hiding," said the Sheik, so calmly and casually as he made himself comfortable on my camel-hide sofa that it could only have been the truth. "I can tell you where he is and how to capture him."

He'd appeared, unannounced, as usual. I knew by the studied, deliberate way he'd extracted a Gauloises from its gold case, examined it, tapped it, lit it, and inhaled and exhaled while he chose his words that whatever he was going to tell me was big.

And indeed, this was a bit of information I didn't think even the Balad bureaucrats would be able to slough off.

Trying to stay casual myself, I came to hyper-alert attention. Not only was this distinguished man the titular Sheik of the Saladin Province, which included the territory from Samarra to Tikrit and all the surrounding Tigris River area, but he had also known Saddam since they were both children. Everything he'd told me so far had proven to be true and of incalculable value, the Abu Seger business being the prime example. I'd heard rumors that the CIA wanted to get their hands on the Sheik. If that were to happen, I knew all too bitterly well what his fate might be.

"Why would you reveal Saddam's whereabouts?" I asked, because I was genuinely curious. "Doing so puts your life in grave danger."

"My life and the lives of my people are already in danger," he answered. "The trouble and complication caused by Saddam's presence in our midst adds exponentially to that danger. I want him out of there." He paused, then added: "Besides, his day is done."

This struck me as the sort of painful yet pragmatic decision a true and skillful leader makes. I believed him. And I could only imagine what it cost him.

"Okay," I said. "What do you have?"

He produced an old map of Saladin province.

"There are eight different hiding places. I can show you the location of each. He moves from one to the other, and I can tell you where he is on any given day." The Sheik smiled. "No more limousines for Saddam," he said. "He travels from hiding place to hiding place in an old rusty taxi."

Was I excited? You probably know how it is when you're in the presence of something real. Talk about the "ring of truth." It was sounding, and it was loud and clear. I'd be out of here soon, I hoped, but with this, perhaps my time in this place would not have been a total waste.

"Wait," I said. "I have an idea." I was thinking of Falconview, an advanced system of aerial mapping and surveillance. I couldn't use it without the approval of my "superiors" down in Balad. I made a call, and got the usual hemming and hawing, foot-dragging, and second-guessing. Here was further affirmation of what I already knew to be true: that the officers in charge were interested in one thing only, and that was the advancement of their own careers. All else was incidental.

"Look," I said to whomever I was talking to on the phone while the Sheik listened with a bemused expression. "Do you or do you not want to capture Saddam Hussein? Isn't he the dictator we supposedly came here to topple? What are we doing? Are we fighting a war, or what?"

I was eventually able to pry permission out of the command down in Balad. I could hardly blame the Sheik for the look on his face.

I brought up Falconview on the computer, entered some coordinates, and showed the Sheik an aerial view of his own home, an ancient Iraqi castle, a.k.a. the Fortress. The view included the chauffeured Mercedes in the driveway, the very Mercedes that sat outside the police station at this moment. The Sheik was duly impressed.

Once he had his bearings, he guided me over to the Tigris River and then north. One by one, the Sheik pinpointed the eight different spots, recognizable to him by the terrain and their positions relative to nearby landmarks.

"These are underground bunkers," he said. "Do not make a move on any of these sites until I take you there. Without me, you will never find him; that's how well camouflaged the bunkers are."

I recorded the exact coordinates of each bunker, and filed this top-secret information, along with the Sheik's admonition, with headquarters in Balad.

The reaction? Nothing. Zilch. Silence. I knew that this non-reaction did not necessarily mean the report had gone unread.

An inner voice told me: *You'd better memorize this.* And I did—all eight sets of the eight-digit coordinates that pinpointed Saddam's location. I used the same memorization technique I'd used when I committed to memory the GSN number on the dispersal door, learned in my agent training, involving linked chains of mnemonic devices. The Saddam coordinates were far more complicated than the GSN number, so I gave it my total concentration. A time would come when I would be glad indeed that I did.

And much later, thousands of miles from Iraq, I would learn that the intelligence I filed, telling them how to catch their top target, the deposed dictator of Iraq, was not only ignored, but laughed at, and quite possibly lost.

# CHAPTER 19

# APPOINTMENT IN SAMARRA

We were feeling pretty good, for a change. The sun was just coming up as we returned to the police station after a pre-dawn prowl. Acting on a tip I'd got the night before, we'd thwarted an ambush. One of my contacts had told me about the planned attack, where it would happen and when, and had drawn a map and a diagram. We caught the guys, no shots were fired, and no one was hurt.

Our high-five mood deflated a few notches when we saw who was waiting for us back at the station: the Dynamic Duo, Maloney and Segura, on one of their surprise drop-ins. This was on the heels of the Sheik's most recent visit.

That morning's successful mission was one of those non-events, that could so easily have been a major event, that you don't hear about, precisely because nothing "happened." But of course, something did happen—lives were saved and a possible conflagration and further mayhem averted.

I told Maloney all about our little victory. I certainly didn't expect a clap on the back or even a "Not bad, Ford," and sure enough, got neither. I did think maybe he'd be a little curious about what had gone down, would show some sort of interest or inquisitiveness in spite of himself, but he didn't. Instead, he watched me with a kind of wariness, as if I were speaking Swahili in an important tone of voice. He looked . . . cornered, embarrassed. The reaction was so peculiar under these circumstances, so out of context, that it was hard to read.

He grunted, then turned and walked off toward the back part of the building.

In the next moment, a sergeant major came in and told me some young Iraqi guy was asking for me out front. Just a little thrown off by my odd encounter with Maloney, I said, oh, okay, and started to head toward the door. The sergeant major grabbed my arm.

"Doc," he said. "The guy asked for you by name. By *name.*"

My antennae were suddenly restored and functioning. Somebody comes and asks for the head intelligence officer by name, and wants him to step outside?

"It's bullshit!" the sergeant major said. "You're not going out there!"

"Jesus Christ. You're right."

"Wait here," said the sergeant. He went out and came back a minute later. "The guy who asked for you is gone."

Of course he was gone. The guy who asked for me was just a tool to lure me out. He wouldn't wait around for the actual event. An eye no doubt peered through the telescopic lens of a rifle on the rooftop of a building, waiting for me. Hot and cold waves coursed along my limbs. And I knew, with a visceral kind of certainty, that death had just missed me by a breath. Somewhere close by was an alternate reality where I lay in the courtyard of the police station, a bullet in my chest. So close that I could still step into that reality if I got careless.

With watery knees, I went back to my office. Behind the closed door to the next room, three voices murmured: Maloney, Segura, and Stavros. They were purposely keeping the volume low so their exact words would be unintelligible. But their agitated tones came through loud and clear.

I sat down at my desk and waited. My hammering heart slowed and my head cooled.

Stavros came out first, with a look on his face like the perp in a *Dragnet* mugshot. He avoided eye contact and moved right on by without a word. Then came Maloney and Segura, both of them acting cagey and fidgety. Segura left without saying anything or glancing in my direction. Maloney stayed, and he was even pissier than usual, as if maybe his panties were a little bunched up. I decided to take the initiative. I mentioned the nearby hospital building, the hissing, dripping bombs within, and the biggest bombshell of them all: that the occupants of that building were Al Qaeda. I was merely reiterating the report I sent in on the day of that encounter, so I knew Maloney knew all of this already, though of course I'd never got any acknowledgment or response.

I watched him carefully as I spoke, curious to see his reaction. He, too, avoided looking at me. What was I detecting in the manner of all three? I couldn't help but wonder if they'd been just a little bit surprised to find me alive and breathing when they stepped through that door. Maloney's aggressive peevishness felt like a cover. An offensive defense.

"Big deal," he said. "I hear this stuff all the time."

"And the Sheik's two-week warning? Any thoughts on that?"

"Yeah, right, sure, like that's really gonna happen." Segura came back into the room then. He did his best Joe Friday impression.

"You're out of here," he said. "Pack up. You leave in twenty-four hours."

"Oh, good," I said. "You got my request for a transfer."

"This isn't your idea," he barked. "It's ours."

"Any thoughts on the Sheik's coordinates of Saddam's location?" I asked calmly.

"Oh, man, you really are out there," Segura sneered, and he and Maloney laughed as if it were all a big joke. Never mind that the Sheik's every word so far had been pure gold.

Maloney and Segura left as abruptly as they'd arrived, roaring off back to Balad.

Had the little tête-à-tête behind the closed door been about me? If not directly about me, then about the future of the operations here without me? I was 99 percent certain. There was a strong continuity between the muffled conference and what they said and did when they came out. I think they were covering their surprise. I think I was supposed to be lying dead outside and not sitting in my chair.

Who might have made the plan for my "unfortunate" demise? A war zone, as you can imagine, is the ideal environment for arranging a "hit" and getting away with it—way easier than, say, a suburban neighborhood in Westchester. And there's an inherent liability within counterintelligence, which is that everyone knows everyone else, especially in one's own team—knows individual habits, movements, and vulnerabilities. When one person turns on another, he or she has plentiful tools at his/her disposal to carry out a successful coup, sabotage, blackmail . . . or murder. And if you think it doesn't happen, you're naïve.

Stalin famously did not flinch from killing whoever needed killing, and he didn't flinch from setting his people against one another. Saddam was Stalin's number one fan, and emulated him, especially in how he ran the Mukhabarat. Mahmoud was Mukhabarat. Mahmoud and Stavros were cozy as a couple of snakes. Stavros hated my guts, and there was no love lost between myself and Mahmoud, who was perfectly aware of the strife between Stavros and me. Strife Mahmoud could use to inspire Stavros to act. With me gone, both of them would benefit; Stavros would be "unbound," and Mahmoud would have that much more influence over Stavros and the intel unit in general. And Maloney and Segura would be unlikely to shed tears at the news of my death.

Could I prove any of it? Like the non-event of the ambush we prevented, this was the non-event of my murder. But all the pieces were in place and fit together with disturbing ease. Mahmoud had slipped into our midst and colonized us. It was not difficult to picture Mahmoud's lips close to Stavros' ear, titillating him with the thrill of a bold proposition, the low, flattering, reassuring tone, as if he spoke to an equal, planting a suggestion here, a hint there, accompanied by a shrug of the shoulders and a raised eyebrow, perhaps offering assistance in recruiting the players among the Iraqi population.

No, I couldn't prove it. But I *knew* it.

It was another moment of epiphany for me, as I grasped, finally and forever, the futility—and now, the mortal danger—of warning, informing, or trying in any way to penetrate the willful, smug, and altogether criminal complacency of my command. I was only too happy to leave Samarra, especially with what I knew was coming. But my worries went beyond concern for my own hide.

A familiar foreboding set in. A freshly sickening conviction presented itself: *I can't trust my fellow countrymen. The Iraqis are far more trustworthy than the Americans.*

With the memory of Abu Seger's fate still fresh and vivid in my mind, I put the word out to all of my assets: *I'll soon be gone. You must never come back to the police station. I don't want you risking your lives any further.*

News got to the Sheik that I was leaving, and he appeared in his black Mercedes.

I was grateful to see him, but I knew that he in particular needed to hear my warning. I was completely frank with him. I spoke to him in private.

"You are unappreciated," I said, urgently, not whispering, but keeping my voice discretely down, "and you could lose your life. You must protect yourself. I can't guarantee your safety. I don't trust these people at all. I don't think they'd hesitate to disappear anyone inconvenient to them. They will stop at nothing."

The Sheik gave me a long, deep look, not unlike the look Abu Seger gave me when we said good-bye for the last time in Tikrit. It was a look that spoke of brotherhood that transcended nationality, tribe, and creed. We both knew we would never see each other again.

We shook hands, he turned, left the station, climbed into his Mercedes, and was gone.

It was the 24th of June. I packed my duffel bags, including copies of the fifty-two detainee medical reports, and left Samarra. Much later, I would hear a rumor that the Sheik was executed in his own home.

# CHAPTER 20

# J'ACCUSE!

Y ou," I said, addressing Segura, "have been covering up torture and abuse."
I'd barged into his office without ceremony first thing when I got to
Balad. Sgt. Padilla was, as usual, right there by his side. They looked up. For a
split second, I saw the whites of their eyes.

"I don't know a goddamned thing about any of that, Ford," Segura shot back.

"Bullshit," I said. "You know very goddamned well what goes on up there in
Samarra. I was reporting it just about every day. And you and Padilla here heard
the screaming from inside the police station that day we were all standing three
feet from the window. If that gunner up there on the roof heard it, so did you,
and you bloody well know it!"

With this, Segura signaled Padilla. They both left the room, had a fast con-
sultation, and then came back.

And Segura uttered the words that would seal many fates:

"No. Nothing happened. You didn't see anything, you didn't hear anything,
and we weren't there."

In that moment, I snapped.

"All right," I said. "That's it. I'm filing charges. You two might deny you were
there, but that machine gunner up on the roof was a witness. It's not just your
word against mine!"

"Tell you what," Segura said in a tone meant to convey leaderly wisdom. "I'll
give you thirty seconds. Forget this whole thing, no one will say anything about
it, and it'll be as if it never happened."

"I'll save you that thirty seconds," I said, leaning in, both hands on his desk.

"I'm not asking you, I'm telling you: get those idiots *out* of that station in Samarra. They're hurting people, and the whole community's about to blow up! We've been warned! Do it or we're going to have a full-on insurgency!"

Mr. Nice Guy turned into Mr. Attack Dog in the blink of an eye. Segura leapt to his feet and rushed around his desk as if he was going to jump me.

"*You don't tell us what to do!*" he snarled. "*We're* the commanders here!"

At Folsom, I'd been rushed by guys a lot bigger and fiercer than the bantam-weight Segura. I held my ground.

He screeched to a halt and gave me a murderous look, but went back around his desk. Padilla was twitching with eagerness for an order from Segura to take me down.

I could practically see the smoke coming from Segura's ears. And what was the source of his fury? It smelled to me like guilt. He'd been set off by the words "torture" and "abuse." And I thought: *He not only knows there's torture going on, he knows it's not just in Samarra. Something's eating him. I bet he heard the same stuff I did about Abu Ghraib, and he's worried for his own ass.* I leaned in again:

"You think what went on up there wasn't torture? Give me a copy of the Geneva Convention. It defines very clearly what's torture and what's not."

"Hell, no. I'm not giving you a copy of the Geneva Convention!"

I shrugged. "Okay, fine. I'll make a note of that. Answer the charges when I file them." With that, I turned, walked out, went to my tent, wrote up the charges against my command of torture and abuse, filed them, went back to Segura's office, slapped copies of the papers on his desk, and walked out.

On my way back to my tent, I crossed through an off-the-beaten-path area behind the other tents, and happened upon an open-air conference of two: Maloney and Col. Thomas Pappas. It was highly peculiar: though I was in plain view, they were so engrossed that they didn't seem to notice me. I stood there, about ten feet from them, not moving, their voices perfectly clear.

"What the hell are we going to tell Karpinski?" said Pappas.

And Maloney answered: "Don't tell her anything."

What were they talking about? Tell Karpinski *what?* Were they talking about me? The particulars didn't matter. What mattered was that they were conspiring to withhold information from a superior officer. Considering that General Janis Karpinski was Col. Pappas' direct boss, this was intent, clearly stated, to commit flagrantly illegal dereliction of duty. And I'd just heard it, loud and clear, with my own ears.

They still seemed not to have noticed me standing a few feet away from them. *Or if they did,* I thought, *they're so far gone in their arrogance that they don't think it matters.* I just sort of melted back and kept moving toward my tent.

Later, I was on my way to consult a legal officer, a guy who'd been sympathetic to my cause, when Segura and Padilla came after me. They blocked my way and ordered me to give up all my weapons, including my beloved Swiss Army knife. I knew that even the slightest move of resistance on my part would have me on the ground, boot on my neck and quite possibly a bullet in my head, so I calmly complied.

I looked Segura in the eye, silently conveying to him that he was making a huge blunder, as I handed over my guns and knives. They demanded my flak vest, too. So not only was I disarmed in a combat zone—which was highly illegal—but I now had zero protection. *It's as if they hope someone will kill me,* I thought. *Fine, though. Here's another crime to add to the charges.* Soon enough, the list of war crimes on the part of my command would steadily accrue in ways that I could not have imagined.

Next, Segura assigned an armed "escort," a Delta Force commando, to follow me everywhere I went. For my "protection," I was told, but I knew this guy was also under orders to report my every move back to Segura and Maloney. Trailed by my "protector," I went to the communications tent and called my lawyer in Sacramento, Judge Advocate General Kevin Healey of the California National Guard, and told him the whole sorry tale. And I told Kevin to contact the Southwest Asia commander, General Stanley McCrystal, and tell him what was going down and why. Kevin was shocked, told me to hang in there, that he'd be making that call, and others, right away.

The next day, I was summoned to Segura's office.

"Okay, Ford. We're granting you 'whistleblower' status," he said with a magnanimous air.

"Fine," I answered. "Put that in writing."

Segura looked insulted. "What, you don't trust me?"

"I'll trust you when I see something on paper and signed by you," I said, and left, my guard right behind me.

A couple of hours later, I was called back again. Segura had a new plan.

"You'll be seeing the combat psychiatrist tomorrow morning. Her name is Capt. Pia Navarro."

"The hell I am."

"We'll take you by force if we have to."

"Oh, we're going to play that game, are we?" I answered wearily. By this time I was well beyond any worry about insubordination.

I kept my appointment with Capt. Navarro, meeting her for the first time the next morning. I was startled by her obvious "greenness." Fresh from civilian life, she had zero savvy about how the military works. But she did a comprehensive interview, asking me questions designed to reveal paranoia, delusions, bipolar disorder, and so forth. Our "interview" lasted about an hour, my guard waiting just outside the door. When she was done, she closed her notebook and looked at me.

"There's nothing wrong with you. You're perfectly lucid."

"Well," I half-joked, "thank you, I guess."

"I'm sure when I report my findings to the command that'll be the end of all this."

I shook my head.

"No," I said. "Just wait. They'll come after you." Now she gave me a look as if maybe she should revise her opinion that I was perfectly sane.

I was right, though. When Navarro delivered her medical opinion to Maloney and Segura, they called a hasty meeting. With eight other medical people present, and with my own 1st Sergeant, Jim Giordano (not his real name), also attending, Segura confronted Navarro. Giordano gave me the eyewitness account right after, and it was a doozy.

Segura, Jim told me, did not pass "go," but went into full-on offense mode right off the bat. Short though he was, he towered over the petite Navarro.

"Your report is *unacceptible*," he'd said, getting right in her face like a drill sergeant so that she flinched backward. Seeing her reaction, he revved it up. "*We're* dictating his treatment!" he shouted, spittle flying. "This is not a *medical* issue. It's an *intelligence* issue. You get him the hell *out* of here. Make up any reason you want. Or else we'll get *you* out of here!"

Jim watched Navarro crumple under the force of Segura's threats. He also saw stunned disbelief on the faces of everyone in the room. Some of them had been in the military a long time, and they'd never seen anything like this. Technically, as an MD in a situation where a medical decision was being made, Navarro had the power to override Segura, but she seemed to not know it. She was, Jim told me, utterly cowed.

"And you didn't hear it from me," Jim said, "but they're going to ransack your bags for documents."

Jesus! Of course! I thanked Jim, then headed directly to the DHL center and shipped the fifty-two copies of detainee medical reports back home to Kevin Healy. I included another precious document: the Carlyle bill of lading that had found its way into my pocket the day I discovered the booby-trapped bomb in the shack at the air base.

———

Within an hour, Maloney came strutting up to me, Segura smirking behind him.

"Well, Ford," he said, "here's the deal. There's something really wrong with you. We're gonna get you the best possible treatment. Go pack your things."

I did, gladly, but sure enough, before I was put into the vehicle that would take me to the airfield, Segura and Padilla seized my bags and tore them apart while I watched calmly. They were deeply pissed when they found nothing. Except, of course, the little love note I'd put in the bag just for them, saying: *Reports shipped home.* A little poem was forming in my head: *Roses are red, violets are blue, reports shipped home, soon I'll be, too.*

They stormed away, leaving my clothing and gear strewn on the ground. I repacked, taking my time.

I was hustled into the waiting vehicle, and delivered, still under guard, to the runway and the Medevac plane, rear doorway open, loaded with wounded soldiers, engines turning, waiting for its one last passenger.

# CHAPTER 21

# WITCH'S BREW

**C**ome sit with me," Navarro said after she unstrapped me from the stretcher she'd ordered me to lie down on before I could board the plane. "I have something to tell you. Something I'll deny if I'm ever asked about it."

She looked at me with big dark eyes as she spoke, her voice lowered though no one was near us. We were still on the ground, moving toward takeoff.

"This had better be good," I said.

"Col. Maloney is the one who arranged all of this. He had to get you out of the country fast as he could, by any means he could. He's scared to death of everything you're saying."

I could see she was in great turmoil, but I had little sympathy.

"You realize," I said to her, "what's going on here, don't you? I don't have any orders. That makes this a rendition. You know what that is, right?" She looked frightened, as if she didn't know the full implication of the term but had a good idea of its gravity.

I looked at her. "Another word for rendition is abduction. As in kidnapping." I let that word sink in. "Kidnapping is a felony. You've made yourself an accessory."

She got up abruptly and hurried away from me. *Good luck,* I thought, but didn't say. *You're going to need it.*

It was a short flight to Camp Virginia in Kuwait, perhaps fifteen minutes. The landing was rough, the plane hitting the runway with a jolt, way too hard, especially with its cargo of wounded soldiers. *Whoa! What the hell is up with you, buddy?* I thought, mentally addressing the pilot. I didn't think of that cowboy landing as any kind of omen, but maybe I should have.

On the ground, we went to a nearby medical tent. I was pretty close to exhaustion; since Maloney and Segura had appeared in Samarra, I'd caught only occasional snatches of ragged, shallow sleep. I lay down on a cot, too buzzed to actually do anything more than just try to rest my bones.

I watched Navarro, at the foot of the cot, filling out a form. She was in the midst of writing when she was abruptly called away. She went, but left the form behind.

Two nurses came into the tent. One of them picked up the form, read it, and visibly froze. She looked at me.

"Are you Ford? The guy she's writing about here?"

"That's me."

"You might want to see this."

One look at the form and any possible shred of sympathy I might have entertained for Navarro evaporated.

She directly contradicted her earlier assessment back in Balad that I was perfectly lucid and normal: "Bipolar disorder?? Medication recommended." it said, followed by her signature.

"I'm going to leave the room now," the nurse who'd called my attention to the form said, doing everything short of winking. She left, I slipped the form out from under the clip and into my shirt pocket then lay back down and closed my eyes. Navarro came back to the tent. Weirdly enough, she did not ask what happened to the medical form she was just filling out. I watched her through half-closed eyes, and immediately detected a change in her manner in the short time she was gone. She was distracted, tight-lipped, and avoided looking at me.

Once again, I was strapped down and loaded onto a second plane, my commando still with me. When we were airborne, Navarro appeared, this time with an assistant, a psych-tech named Jon Weber (not his real name) I was expecting to be released from my bonds, like last time, but she didn't say a word and was still avoiding eye contact when she took me totally by surprise, plunging a hypodermic needle deep into the muscle of my arm. Within seconds, I was weak, rubbery, and woozy. *Valium,* I thought, while I could still think. Then, with Bauer's assistance, she stuck an IV into the vein inside my elbow. Drugged and restrained, I was unable to put up any resistance. I had but a moment of seeing liquid move down the IV line, and then it was swirling, blackout oblivion.

Consciousness dawned after what could only have been many hours. I fought my way up through a kaleidoscopic haze, struggling to orient myself. I was a pinpoint of awareness with no name, no history, and no identity. I was alone. *Where am I? Who am I?* I knew I was on an airplane, and that it was daytime, but that was all I knew. I rolled my aching cannonball-heavy head from side to side, trying to shake things loose.

Memories began to crowd and jostle.

And I thought: *Did I dream it? Iraq, the WMD, the burn pits, the Sheik, Abu Seger, tortured prisoners, Rudi the Desert Dog, mortar fire and explosions, piles of money, the Pink Palace, the melted radio truck, the grotesquely wounded people and soldiers, the medical reports, Maloney and Segura, the fruitless attempts to make my command pay attention to the disaster they'd fostered—all just a long bad dream, and now I'm waking up?*

I tried to rise, but found myself bound like Gulliver. With a great straining effort, I was able to contort myself and reach a knife stashed in my boot. I wasn't a fool—I hadn't handed over all my weapons to Segura and Padilla. I was able to cut myself loose, sit up, and look out the window.

The plane happened to be passing over one of the ultimate distinctive landmarks of the world, the Rock of Gibralter. The sight of it—iconic, monolithic, timeless—solidified reality for me in an instant, and I snapped to full awareness. I knew exactly where I was, and as the plane turned northeast, I knew where I was headed: Germany.

Iraq, sadly, was no dream. I remembered it all now, including everything that put me on that plane. At the same moment, another memory materialized from the last few hours, one I did not for even a moment mistake for a dream—faces, bent over me, asking questions: "Who did you call? Who did you contact?" And I recalled specific words: "What do you know about Copper Green? Who did you speak to about it?" And I knew: I wasn't supposed to remember them interrogating me, but I did. Whatever mix they gave me in that IV was supposed to loosen my tongue and wipe out my memory. But they didn't realize who they were messing with.

I always had an excellent memory, and it had been trained and cultivated in my various professions. I tested myself now, calling up the coordinates of Saddam's hiding places. The numbers popped onto the screen of my mind, clear and intact, twinkling like Christmas lights, as if to say: *Here we are, boss!*

Why, I wondered, was I alone? Even my Delta Force commando, close as a shadow for the last couple of days, was not there. Eventually, I'd find out why Navarro and Weber were absent: because they were in the cockpit, being grilled via radio by German authorities, who'd heard that there was someone aboard this flight against his will. This was of grave concern to the Germans, ever making amends for WWII. They are understandably more sensitive to war crimes than other nationalities and do not fool around when it comes to even a hint of impropriety on their soil. Navarro and Weber, I would learn, simply denied everything: Oh, no, nobody's being coerced here. We're doctors. Everything's fine.

How did the Germans know I was on that plane? Later, I would learn that my phone call to my JAG lawyer, Kevin Healy, who'd followed through and contacted General McCrystal, had probably saved my life. Anticipating my forced removal, Kevin had specified to McCrystal that I would likely be put on a Medevac flight to Germany, against my will, that the Germans should be notified, and most important of all, that I not arrive in a body bag, but vertical and breathing, or heads would roll.

Technically, they were creating an international incident with every lie coming from their mouths, not to mention every drug pumped into my veins. Their crimes compounded. Soon the plane was touching down at the American Air Force base in Landstuhl, Germany. I disembarked under my own power, Navarro never asking how I got loose or checking on my condition. My Delta Force commando, who'd left me alone while I was unconscious and tied down, was with me again. We rode a bus to the terminal, and went in together. He left me alone for a few minutes while he checked in, then came back into the room.

"Jesus," he said, recoiling a little. "Do you know how bad we smell?" I was too preoccupied to notice any aroma, or maybe I was inured to it. But he'd just had a breath of fresh German air and then returned to the small closed room where I waited for him. "We smell like incinerated dead bodies and burnt raw sewage."

What he was describing was the burn-pit smell, clinging to us like sin, a bad conscience or an old regret. Not that my uniform was filthy—it wasn't. It's that we were permeated, from our hair down to our boots, with the crime that was the war in Iraq.

The guy's duty was over. Now he'd go back. Before he turned to take his leave, he shook my hand and looked at me with real sympathy

"I've never seen such shit in my life," he muttered, and was gone.

# CHAPTER 22

# TERRA FIRMA

You're making accusations of war crimes," said the doctor. "Did you tell your officers about these war crimes?"

I could hardly believe my ears.

"Tell my officers? Who do you think put me on that plane?" I said, a little sharply, thinking: *you condescending young pup!*

Now he had an almost happy look on his face.

"So you're saying they arranged for you to be abducted?"

I answered without hesitation: "That's correct." And I watched, reading upside down, as the doctor wrote in his notes: Delusions, paranoia.

This guy was the first doctor I met with on the ground in Landstuhl. He was young and gung-ho, with a hungry look in his eye. He was sizing me up like prey before the interview even began. When I gave him my account, he was practically licking his chops.

I just sighed. *So be it,* I thought.

It was a little different with the next doc. This one, Dr. Tsai, was much older, had plainly been at this for a long, long time and had seen a thing or two. He took a look at Navarro's latest medical report on me. He shook his head incredulously.

"Where's she getting this shit? Did she copy it out of DSM4?" That's shorthand for the *Diagnostic and Statistical Manual for Mental Disorders,* not exactly a page-turner. I told the whole story again, from the prisoner abuse I witnessed to ignored intelligence to disappearing mountains of money to being renditioned, forced onto the plane, and drugged. "In our biz," said Tsai, "a diagnosis of 'Bipolar Disorder' opens the door to an entire inventory of further diagnoses and justifications for 'treatment.' It's what you say when you don't know what else to say, but you want to sound official. This is a perfect bullshit example." And he looked at me. "You don't want to go back, do you?"

"If I did, you'd be right to call me crazy," I joked.

"It's obvious you're not crazy. You're more than fit to serve. But if I send you back there, your life will be worth nothing. You won't survive. So I'm sending you home." He made some notations, then sighed. "Thank God I'm retiring."

And there it was, conspicuous by its absence in this older doc: naked self-interest, the vein that ran through this whole sorry enterprise, from the lies that fueled the invasion to the mercenary drive of everyone from high government officials with a stake in reaping giant profits to the officers with their "Six-Figure-Salary" mantra to the ambitious young doc who'd interviewed me first. Unlike the young doc, this man was nearing the end of his professional career and was not thinking only of his next promotion. He had no reason to be anything but honest, and his honest assessment of me was that I was anything but crazy. His manner suggested that this was not the first time he'd seen someone go against the prevailing grain and be railroaded for his efforts.

The next morning, after the first good night's sleep I'd had in many a day, I ran into Navarro and Weber in the dining hall. I was feeling way better, and keenly relishing the prospect of home. Poor Navarro, though, looked keel-hauled; her hands jerked and shook, her eye-whites flashed, and she mumbled a few words but no complete sentences. I know terror when I see it, and I thought to myself: *You look as if you got slapped around by a really big boogeyman.* Weber, on the other hand, seemed pretty relaxed, and proposed that we all take a nice boat trip up the Rhine the next day. In a magnanimous mood, I said, sure, why not? And I thought: *We'll have to keep an eye on Navarro in case she decides to jump overboard.*

But it was not to be. Navarro and Weber got their orders the next morning to return to Iraq. The boat ride was cancelled. *Sayonara,* I thought. I did not envy them.

Soon I was aboard a military flight for the United States. During the flight, I fell into conversation with an elderly ex-military couple sitting next to me.

"My husband and I have been watching you," said the woman, "and we believe you've been to war. Are we right?" I gave them a rueful smile.

"Does it show?" I joked.

The couple, who were African-American, told me that they left the United States a long time ago and now lived in Italy, in the lovely little cliffside village of Positano on the southward western coast. They told me about the perfect weather, the pastel-colored houses, the delectable food, the kind, non-racist people, the ancient steep streets, the ridiculously reasonable cost of living, and the soothing breezes blowing in off the Mediterranean.

"You need to come there and live," said the husband. "It'll heal your soul."

I was profoundly touched, both by their wonderful human concern and by the images they conjured. And I knew they were right. *Soul healing,* I thought. *That's exactly what I need.*

We landed at Andrews at dawn, June 30, 2003. There would be a delay before we could disembark, because nearby, a military plane, a C5A, had landed. I and a lot of others on our plane had an unobstructed view.

The rear hatch of the C5A was open, and a full honor guard stood at attention as the plane's cargo was unloaded: four flag-draped coffins. There was a crowd—reporters, TV cameras, politicians, and military officers. I watched through the window along with most of my fellow passengers, all of us in a state of hushed awe as word spread about what we were witnessing. The four coffins were those of some of the first soldiers confirmed killed by IEDs in Iraq, right near Samarra, four men who might be alive today if my command had heeded my urgent warning from the Sheik: *They're going to pack the culverts with explosives.*

Watching the sad ceremony, I thought bitterly: *I gave them everything they needed to prevent this, and they laughed it off. Are they laughing now?*

# CHAPTER 23

# AMBER WAVES
# OF GRAIN

Man, I can't tell you how good it felt to be back on American soil. I flopped down on a gurney in the medical waiting area and relaxed deeply into some sorely-needed shut-eye, knowing I'd be getting on another plane soon: next stop, Fort Sam Houston in San Antonio, Texas.

A few hours later, I was aboard and eight miles high, getting an informal welcome-home tour of the good old US of A as the military flight took a round-about route to Texas, going first to Minnesota and Oklahoma and various other far-flung stops. This was perfectly fine with me. I was so glad to be home that I thoroughly enjoyed the meandering trip and the sights from way up in the sky. Here was the antidote to the Middle East blues and its endless desert-scape. I was feeling tender and sentimental in spite of it all.

Word must have got out, because during the flight various members of the crew came back to ask me questions. When I told each of them my story, they responded with similar stories of their own from their time in the Middle East, of incidents of torture and/or abuse they either witnessed or heard rumors about, and how they, too, were told not to talk about it. It was gratifying to not only be believed, but to know that I wasn't alone. Not that I was happy to learn that torture, abuse, and cover-up were so common, but there was vindication in knowing that what I'd seen were scarcely isolated incidents. That it was, in fact, part of a general sickness.

Arriving at last at San Antonio, I was taken to the Ft. Sam medical facility for a psych evaluation. I was struck by the contrast between the reception here and the one I got in Germany. With the exception of Dr. Tsai, everyone I encountered over there had been eager to discredit me, paint me as a crazed lunatic, and otherwise cover up and bury what I had to say about war crimes.

If a name can be a portent, I was well pleased with name of the first person I officially encountered—Major Lorenzo Lucky, an MD, who took a look at my papers and immediately asked me to tell my story. He listened attentively, did not make insinuations about paranoia or delusions, and spoke thoughtfully when I finished.

"This is going on right now? We've been suspecting something like this was happening, but you're the first one to put it so lucidly, clearly, and consistently. Come with me." And he took me to a psychiatrist named Robert Hardaway, filling him in on my ordeal.

Like Dr. Tsai, Dr. Hardaway was on the brink of retiring and so had no ambitious agenda. He exuded humor, equanimity, and an air of having seen it all. It seemed that it was obvious to him, too, that I was not "crazy." And like Major Lucky, he listened respectfully and attentively. He was disgusted with the behavior of my command and the sadists under them as per my report, and said he'd recommend that an investigation into the charges be launched ASAP.

Hardaway escorted me directly upstairs to the office of the Inspector General (IG), another guy with an auspicious name: Col. Mercury. Again, I was treated to full credulity. Col. Mercury asked if my command had responded in any way to the charges.

"Only to deny everything and to smear me any way they could," I said. "As you can see in the memo they wrote. Saying they'd never condone torture, calling me crazy and all the rest of it." We were looking at the rush-job response to the charges I filed in Balad, Maloney and Segura putting their noggins together and coming up with a throw-it-against-the-wall-and-see-what-sticks mish-mash. They said, for instance, that my claim to have worked with the Nixon security detail was nothing but a tall tale, and the same with my claim to Native American ancestry.

If these geniuses had checked my background security clearance, they would have seen that all of my "claims," from my ancestry to being part of the Nixon detail, were certified genuine. It didn't occur to them to do that, and it didn't occur to them how it would make them look when anybody else checked my background.

I watched Col. Mercury's jaw set as I spoke.

"Okay," he said. "I'm going to create a full set of charges. We'll submit them immediately to the Inspector General of the Department of Defense in Washington DC, requesting a formal investigation."

I was beyond gratified. *Smooth sailing so far,* I thought. *Maybe this won't be so difficult after all.*

You'd think I'd have learned one of life's iron laws by then: things can always take a turn.

Who was the director of the Office of the Inspector General of the Department of Defense upon whose desk the report of torture and abuse by the 205th Military Intelligence Brigade landed? None other than George W. Bush's close friend and appointee, Joseph E. Schmitz, who, in the near future, would be forced to resign under allegations of obstructing an FBI investigation into contract improprieties and war crimes in Iraq, and who, after his resignation, would go to work for Blackwater.

Smooth sailing soon gave way to troubled waters . . .

# CHAPTER 24

# HEAL THYSELF

So. When did you decide to join the Mukhabarat and plot against the United States?" Hardaway deadpanned.

I gaped at him for about a tenth of a second, then understood. "Brace yourself," he went on. "You're not going to believe what they're saying about you." Hardaway paused. "I take that back. Of course you're going to believe it. What you might not believe is how fast they're doing it."

"Lay it on me," I sighed.

"They're accusing you of treason. They're saying you gave away sensitive intelligence to one of your assets, who relayed it to the Mukhabarat. Does 'Operation Serpent' mean anything to you?"

*Richter,* I thought. *Talk about a snake.* And I remembered the day in Samarra when he walked in on a meeting I was in the midst of with the Sheik. We'd been discussing a plan by the Mukhabarat to stage a shock-and-awe operation that would happen at the same time as our own multi-city operation, code named Operation Serpent, which would be simultaneous lightning attacks on Fallujah and Samarra with the intent of putting down the insurgency. Before Richter came into the room, the Sheik had made it plain from what he said that he knew all about Operation Serpent already, had used the very words. Richter came in, sat down, and heard me use the phrase Operation Serpent in my response to the Sheik. He left the room shortly thereafter, looking a little stiff and wary.

Now I was learning that he'd decided he'd caught me being a traitor, had obviously gone straight to Maloney and Segura with this big hot scoop, and that they'd filed it away for future use. Now they were cashing in their chips, or so they thought. It was a reflection of the sorry state of our operation in Samarra that I couldn't trust a member of my own team; looking back, I realized I should have tossed Richter out of the room as soon as he put his big foot through the door. Of course, he was eager to get back at me; he knew he was on the list of abusers I'd complained about to the command.

This was my second day at Ft. Sam Houston, and I was meeting with Drs. Lucky and Hardaway. I'd been hopeful when I arrived there that morning. Now that hope was a little less shiny. Dr. Lucky apologized for the lousy treatment I was getting, and Hardaway warned me that I should expect these sorts of lies and distortions.

"Be ready for it to get worse," he said darkly. "This is what they do." And Hardaway gave me a few days' leave. The Fourth of July was coming up. "Go home, have fun, relax," he said.

I did just that. I flew to California, went to a friend's horse ranch where rolling hills, beautiful scenery, ponds, old oak trees, a barbecue, and best of all, hundreds of happy people went a long way toward healing my soul.

Refreshed and restored, I headed back to San Antonio, expecting to be discharged and to put the military behind me once and for all.

But it was not to be. When I got back to San Antonio, I learned that Maloney, Segura, and Pappas were raising ever more hell in response to the charges. They were not only accusing me of treason, they were doubling down on their denial that any WMD were found, nor money beneath Abu Seger's house, saying again I'd invented everything, that I was insane, delusional, and out to get them. I was advised to stay at least in reserve status so the Three Amigos didn't wriggle out through some loophole, and so that the CID (Criminal Investigation Division) and/or the IG didn't drop my case, which they could do if I were a civilian. They'd likely be looking for any excuse, I was advised, and that would be right at the top of the list.

*God damn,* I thought as I reluctantly agreed. *Where's this going to end?* I went home to Sacramento, and immediately marched into the headquarters of the California National Guard (CNG). I demanded that their legal officer, Col. Nathaniel Quentin (not his real name), file an official request for an investigation, plus charges, this time from the CNG itself.

Col. Quentin listened to my story. His stance was one of mildly condescending concern for me and my complaints—about WMD, torture, illegal rendition, and the complicity of my command in the denials and cover-ups thereof—with an overlayer of cool skepticism. And he made it quite clear that his first priority was to defend the command, not to defend me.

But I successfully got his attention when I mentioned the dispersal door from the VX canister and the GSN stamped on it. The notion of tangible evidence supporting one of my major claims—that a huge stash of WMD of American origin had been found and the discovery concealed from the world, the evidence destroyed—caused a major change in his attitude. Now that he knew I might actually have something irrefutable against the command he was so devoted to protecting, he had to do more than just speak vague, mollifying words to me.

"I want that dispersal door," he said.

"Well, Colonel," I said, "you'll have to ask Col. Maloney about that. The last I saw the thing, it was on his desk in Balad. What I do have, though, is that number, that GSN that's stamped on it. You can check it out yourself."

With that, I had the satisfaction of watching the man's expression go from cynical to astonished to persuaded that what I had to say was worthy of his attention. Because if what I said checked out, then his job of defending the command just got a lot more complicated. Included in that complication, I figured, would be the necessity to protect himself from being part of an ongoing cover-up. He was in a hell of a pickle. Damned if he did, damned if he didn't.

"Okay," said Quentin. "Okay. I'm going to call the CID and we'll file. And we'll let them know that a report has gone to the IG."

By then, of course, the charges had compounded. They included not only the original charges I handed to Segura back in Iraq—naming him, Maloney, Stavros, May, and Richter as torturers and/or aiders and abettors—but now also charges of my forcible abduction and drugging by Maloney and Segura, with Navarro's name prominently added. Ironically enough, it would be the charges involving the abrogation of my rights, now appended to the original charges of prisoner abuse and torture in Iraq, which would eventually impel the case upward through the various courts as they tossed it like the proverbial hot potato. By now, I'd learned about the Lincoln Law and that it most certainly applied to the vanished money found under Abu Seger's house. I added to the charges a claim for 20 percent of that.

The very next day, I got a call from the command, demanding to know why I wasn't in Ft. Lewis, up in the state of Washington.

"We're going to get a set of orders for you to go up there ASAP!"

I got a big kick out of twitting them a little:

"I'd like to see you do that," I said, "seeing as technically, I'm still in Iraq." There was some harrumphing and dissembling, but the orders did come through.

So off I went, up to Ft. Lewis. This was not, all things considered, such a bad place to tread water for a while as a reservist. It's near the Puget Sound, and so there was the sea, salmon fishing, and proximity to wilderness. I enrolled in a firefighting course. I got plenty of rest, and friends came to visit. It was all excellent "therapy." It might not have been Positano, but it was soul-healing. I was in a sort of "holding" unit; my guess was that the command hoped to keep me as incommunicado as they could. It would also turn out that Maloney was trying to fudge things so that my exact whereabouts would be hazy. Apparently, he wanted to maintain the numerical headcount of his "manning roster" for the sake of appearance, letting it be thought that I was still in Iraq. Which he knew he could do because of the lack of any official orders to the contrary. Maloney's crimes were growing exponentially like the proverbial pond algae.

When I first got there, I was called into a captain's office. I went, expecting the worst. The captain, a woman, sat me down and asked some pointed questions.

"Who are you, and how did you wind up here under my command, with no orders?" I told her the whole story, and I could see her face clouding as I revealed the details. When I was done, she stood up abruptly. *Uh-oh,* I thought; *I've pissed her off. She's gonna throw me out of her office or something.*

Instead, she shook my hand.

"Thank you for what you're doing," she said. "This is some of the most courageous, heroic action I've ever seen." And she told me that she herself had been deployed to combat zones and had seen horrific treatment of prisoners, felt helpless to do anything about it, and saw the fear of everyone around her to do anything about it. "What I saw were war crimes," she affirmed. "Just as what you saw were war crimes."

Not long after, I had a similar experience with another officer, a major at the military hospital there. This guy, too, asked me how I got there with no orders. I told my story yet again, and got listened to with great attention and then thanked profusely for taking action where others would not.

And again, I learned that I was scarcely alone. I heard the story of Lt. Julian Goodrum, a platoon commander with the 212 Transportation Unit in Iraq in 2003. Their job was to drive a convoy of huge trucks carrying everything from tanks to air conditioners to generators to port-a-potties and anything else you can think of to far flung locations around Iraq to serve the war effort. He was shocked by the lethal deficiencies of the unit's equipment and supplies—old rattletrap unarmored trucks that might break down at any moment (and did), crude hand-drawn maps, no radios, no intel about danger points along their remote, lonely routes, and insufficient ammunition, all of it putting his people in grave danger. He complained to his command, in vain.

Constant vigilance wore him down, and he soon developed PTSD, like everyone around him, but his worse because he was in charge. Wrist injuries caused him to be evacuated back to the States after a few months of this grueling duty. He was home, waiting for medical treatment, frustrated with delays and bureaucracy, when he heard that one of his men in the 212, someone he knew well, was killed in a gruesome accident when the brakes of the truck he was driving failed and he was crushed between his vehicle and the one in front. Goodrum's PTSD flared up acutely at the news of this completely preventable death. His immediate superior in Iraq, to whom he'd complained about the shoddy equipment, immediately started a cover-up, blaming the dead man.

Goodrum had never filed a formal complaint against the military before, but now he did, specifically naming that superior officer.

He quickly found himself the object of a smear campaign. His superior officer and others did their best to frame him as a drug dealer and a deserter. He was also falsely diagnosed as "crazy" and forced into psychiatric lockdown. The effort to shut him up was sloppy—a tangle of forged documents, contradictions, and outright lies—but Goodrum was forced to spend tens of thousands of dollars defending himself. The only charge they were able to make stick was a vague and flimsy one, "fraternization" with a female soldier. He was left bitter, disillusioned, in debt, and suicidal. I knew exactly how he felt.

And there was devastation and grotesque tragedy. I had noticed a woman at Ft. Lewis. I'd seen her in the dining room and here and there on the grounds. She was quiet, withdrawn, and obviously brooding. She was recently back from the Middle East; the rumor was that she had seen "some bad stuff" in Iraq. I'd met this woman, spoken with her a little. One day about a week after her arrival, she took a kitchen knife and slashed her wrists and cut her own throat when she was alone in her quarters. She bled out. The forensic people who'd inspected the scene, not sure at first if they had a murder or a suicide on their hands, said that the "splatter pattern" of arterial blood on the walls made it plain that she had walked around and around her room before she died.

At about the same time, around July 9, news came in from Samarra—someone had driven a VBED (Vehicle Bomb Explosive Device), another way of saying truck bomb, through the front door of the police station, levelling it. People were killed. Just before the VBED, an IED was planted at the gate, and blew up a vehicle carrying May and some others. None of them died, but they could have. It was sheer luck they sustained only relatively minor injuries. I have no doubt that this "team" was precisely who the "insurgents" were after. Later, I found out that May got a Purple Heart for getting some shrapnel in the attack. It all happened just about two weeks from the day the Sheik gave me the two-week warning. Once again, the Sheik, my old friend I knew I'd never see again, had been spot-on.

Did anyone acknowledge that I was right, that the Sheik's intel, as always, was completely accurate? Did anyone thank me for the timely warning and the valuable work? Not only were no thanks forthcoming, but the out-and-out efforts to sabotage me began in earnest.

# CHAPTER 25

# FORKED TONGUES

I have the coordinates to Saddam's location stored in a safe place," I said. "Up here." And I pointed to my head.

The pleasant young CID officer I was speaking to, Kevin Lohan (not his real name), reacted a lot the way I did when the Sheik told me he knew where Saddam was hiding. He looked up from his paperwork and came to sharp attention.

"That's not the only place they're stored, though, right?"

"Your guess is as good as mine. I sent the intel off to Balad the same day I got it."

"And . . . ?"

"And nothing." I shrugged.

It was late November. I was still at Ft. Lewis, and I'd gone to the CID office there to check on the progress of my case. In the course of briefing him on the details, I'd told him about the Sheik and our many conversations, including the bombshell about Saddam. Lohan was flabbergasted at the flippant attitude of my command.

"But that's vital information for the war effort!" Lohan said.

"No kidding," I replied.

"We need to alert the 902nd about those coordinates."

"Fine," I agreed. "Go ahead." The 902nd was US Military Intelligence.

He said that in the meantime, he'd initiate a series of checks to see if any action was being taken on my case. He didn't waste any time, and he wasn't just blowing smoke. I was still there in the room when he began doing just that.

Next day, the phone rang.

"Do you have any idea how hot you are right now?" It was Lohan.

"No," I joked. "How hot am I?"

"I called Counterintelligence about the Saddam coordinates. They want to talk to you."

It so happened Kathy was with me, up from Sacramento for a visit. She agreed to come along as a witness.

A smart decision, as it turned out.

We drove across the base to the 902nd headquarters, where we met up with Lohan and were escorted to a bunker. As we went in, the prickly little warning hairs along my arms stirred, and I experienced a gut-level sense of danger, not unlike the moment on the base in Balad when I was about to enter the booby-trapped hut. You learn to trust that feeling.

An Agent Johnston (not his real name) met us inside. He did not introduce himself or say good morning or even rise from his chair. He looked at me with an opaque expression, then spoke like a high school principal to a juvenile delinquent.

"What's this about the location of Saddam?"

I started to tell him about getting this vital intel from the Sheik in Samarra, that I'd reported it, and that the Sheik's info had always been pure gold.

"Yeah, yeah," he interrupted rudely. "But what's all this about some numbers you have?"

Now the sense of danger kicked up a notch or two.

"I'm getting a creepy feeling," I said. "Why am I talking to you? I was abducted, strapped to a stretcher, drugged, and illegally renditioned out of a war zone because of you people. You know I've launched an investigation into war crimes. I'm betting you've been in touch with my unit, and now you're looking for a way to burn me."

With that, he was out of his seat.

"Wait right here," he barked. He went into another room. Kathy and I looked at each other while we listened to murmuring on the other side of the door. Shades of Segura and Padilla.

Then Johnston was back, slamming the door behind him importantly.

"I'm going to read you your rights," he announced.

*What?*

"Oh, really?" I said, not bothering to keep the contempt out of my voice. I whipped out my phone, speed-dialed Kevin Healy, my Judge Advocate General lawyer, and got him on the line while Johnston was still talking.

"We've decided we're going to book you for all of this," Johnston announced.

"Book me for what?"

"Espionage, of course," said Johnston. "You have the location of Saddam Hussein."

"No," I said. "I don't have the location of Saddam Hussein."

"Well, your unit does."

"So you *were* in touch with my unit, and you spoke to them before you spoke to me?"

Johnston ignored this, and continued.

"According to the CID, you have the eight sets of eight-digit coordinates of Saddam's location, and you carried them out of Iraq."

"Yes," I shot back. "I carried the coordinates out of Iraq—in my head, while I was strapped down, drugged, and transported *against my will*. You call that espionage?"

Johnston glared: "We do. Let's have those coordinates."

"I'm not giving you jack shit!" I said, fury rising. I thrust the phone toward him. "Here, why don't you talk to my lawyer about charging me with espionage? He just heard everything you said."

Johnston pulled back, his face tightening, clearly not liking having the tables turned on him.

"I'm not talking to your goddamned lawyer!"

"Kevin," I said into the phone while I looked at Johnston, "call the commander of the 902nd military intelligence unit and tell them you're going to talk to the southwest Asia commander McCrystal about espionage charges being drawn up against me."

"Okay," Kevin said, on speakerphone so Johnston could hear. "I'm doing it."

With that, Lohan, Kathy, and I walked out.

The next day, Johnston called, using another page from his playbook. Now he sounded like a salesman getting ready to offer me an irresistible deal. He was chummy and conciliatory and spoke as if he had a wonderful surprise waiting for me.

"Come on in," he said. "We just want to talk to you." Reluctantly, Kathy and I went. Now Johnston was exuding magnanimity. This time, there were a couple of people in the office with him. Backup, I guessed. All of them were smiling. Only Johnston spoke.

"We've decided we're gonna cut you a deal," he said. "You filed charges of torture against the team. Tell you what: we'll just read you your rights, and stop there, if you'll drop the charges." I guess he expected me to breathe a big sigh of relief, mop my brow, and thank him.

He had, as they say, another thing coming.

"Do I look stupid? Read me my *rights?* I'll read you *your* rights!"

Johnston was slack-jawed. Plainly, he and his people were not used to anything other than groveling and compliance.

"And I'll tell *you* what," I said in a calm but deadly firm voice. "I'm doubling down on the charges, as a matter of fact. I'm calling my lawyer and making sure that the charges of war crimes are pressed against Stavros and the others, and I'm going to make sure the command gets charged with trying to whitewash those crimes and with arranging for me to be kidnapped and drugged! Oh, and the theft of hundreds of millions of dollars, too. That ought to sweeten the pot. I'm not letting these assbites get away with anything."

Kathy witnessed it all. She, too, could not believe her ears. The looks on the faces of Johnston and his cronies when I defied them were priceless, like the gaping faces of the folks on the old *Candid Camera* show at the moment they realize they've been had: total change of reality in the space of second.

"No deal," I enunciated, as if maybe they didn't speak English too well. With that, Kathy and I walked out. We agreed; these people were completely crazy. Kevin Healy also agreed, and I thought for the hundredth time: *No wonder we're losing this war.*

Wasn't I afraid they'd arrest me right then and there, taze me, or throw a net over me? Possibly, but they'd all been warned already by Kevin not to talk to me unless he was present. So they were on shaky ground themselves when they violated that directive. So they bluffed, and I called them on it.

About a week later, Johnston made one more attempt to "read" me my "rights," but this time, I just ignored him.

Shortly thereafter, in the first week of December, I got a call from Lohan, saying he hoped I'd come in because he had something that he could only tell me in person. I went.

He said he felt bad about how things had gone. As he spoke, he slid a piece of paper across the desk. On it was a phone number.

"You have every right to call these people and give them that intel. It's entirely up to you." I knew he was talking about the Saddam coordinates. I recognized the number as "agency" (CIA), and suspected I would be taken seriously by those at the other end.

I waited for perhaps twenty-four hours and called from a government phone.

"Look," I said to the voice on the other end of the line. "You're still hunting for Saddam. Here's your chance to stop looking like the assholes you are." Yes, I spoke as bluntly as that. I'd had enough dealings with "agency" to know that I could, and should.

I told how I reported the coordinates while I was still in Iraq, but that my report was apparently ignored, and, as I would later learn, probably lost. Then I closed my eyes, called up the memorized numbers and gave them to the contact on the other end of the line. What I did not reveal was my source; to do so would have put my old friend in grave danger. I also remembered the Sheik telling me not to try to find Saddam unless he, the Sheik, was present, but it was too late for that now. I wished them luck, and hung up.

About a week later, Dec. 13, 2003, Lohan called me in again. I went to his office.

He had a huge smile on his face.

"They caught Saddam," he said. "I guess you made that call, eh?"

Now it was my turn to gape. Lohan had delivered the scoop to me before it was released to the world. Within hours, the famous picture of a bearded, bedraggled Saddam, fresh from his "spider hole," flashed 'round the world.

The riddle, of course, was this: Did Johnston have the coordinates all along, as filed by me in Iraq in the company of the Sheik? Or were they actually "lost" or even discarded? If Johnston had them, he could have been trying to lay a snare for me—if I had yielded those memorized coordinates to Johnston, and they matched the original coordinates I filed in Iraq, then the "espionage" trap would be sprung. *Ah-ha! Gotcha!*

More likely, though, is that he did not have them, that they had indeed been lost or discarded, but in the interval between my mentioning the memorized coordinates to Lohan and then Lohan mentioning them to the 902nd, Johnston saw an "opportunity" to get those coordinates back, and contacted my unit— Maloney, Segura, et al—and then, conniving with them, contrived a way to try to make me drop the charges while at the same time covering up the embarrassing "loss" of this vital intel. Drop charges, save face, and put me out of commission.

*Nice try,* I thought.

Not long after I made the call to the agency and Saddam was found in a below-ground bunker, right where the Sheik said he'd be, I learned that Lohan had been demoted and sent to Afghanistan to drive trucks.

# CHAPTER 26

# BAD FAITH

They're rampaging through Abu Ghraib right now," said the young Navy Seal guy next to me on the plane. "They're tearing the place apart." Like Lohan telling me about the capture of Saddam, I got this tectonic scoop way before the world heard about it. This was a preview of coming attractions. The story and images that would fly around the planet were still a few months away.

I wasn't being held prisoner in Ft. Lewis. I'd hopped a military flight to California for a couple of days' R&R. On board the plane, I met the Navy Seal guy. I had been assigned as a medic to the Navy Seals about thirty years before, and so we "bonded" right away and struck up a conversation. It was from this fellow that I heard the first early inside news about the leak of graphic photos of torture at Abu Ghraib. The details would come later. It was now early January 2004.

And there was a cherry on top for me. My new friend added that he saw a show on ABC News, with "some asshole" by the name of Maloney, home on a short leave, being interviewed about prisoner abuse in Iraq and denying everything. I was grimly amused; the Navy Seal guy mentioned Maloney, and his assessment of him, with zero prompting from me.

Abu Ghraib, of course, was only one highly public manifestation of a systemic sickness. Around the same time, I met a young captain from Hawaii, recently back from Iraq, who told me about having witnessed rape, murder, and an elaborate cover-up of it on the part of his countrymen. The young captain seethed with fury at the indifference of those "in charge."

"I know the feeling," I told the guy. "I know the feeling."

Later that January, I left Ft. Lewis for good and went home to Sacramento. I hadn't been home a day when I got a call from a buddy up there:

"You're not gonna believe who just got here and who's standing in front of me right now!"

"Let me guess," I said. "Maloney and his unit?" My guess was right.

"And this prick, Maloney," said my buddy, "he's yelling at everybody, treating them all like shit, threatening them. The people he's been with in a war zone for almost a year! He's a piece of work!" I nearly asked my pal to hand the phone to Maloney, but better judgment prevailed.

Too often, meanwhile, I was about as pleasant to be around as a grizzly bear with a toothache. My temper was short and my sleep bad. Frustrations seethed. This is hardly unusual among those who return from war zones with wounds either visible, not visible, or both. Kathy and I agreed that I would get my own apartment temporarily. It was hardly fair for me to inflict myself on her until some of my rough edges got smoothed off. We were very lucky to have the means to do this; I'm well aware that not everybody does, and there's a lot of damage to innocent bystanders because of it as people and their pain get crowded together in small spaces. In my monastic little apartment, I could hole up, hibernate, and hide out.

I went back to my old job as a corrections officer at Folsom Prison. Kathy and I stayed in close touch, of course. She kept a list and notes of who called the house in the name of "checking up" on me. They didn't know about my hideaway. She'd just tell them I was out, and could she take a message? A lot of suspiciously "concerned" people were trying to ring me up, she told me, asking with fishy solicitude after my wellbeing. Asking if I was getting therapy, how my health was, and so forth. One of the callers was none other than Maloney's wife:

"Is he going to be okay? Is there anything we can do?" she asked, sweet as pie. We agreed that she could only have been put up to this call by Maloney.

Mrs. Maloney's concern was truly touching, considering that soon after that call, I got a notification via FedEx from her husband, telling me my security clearance was being pulled. This was a peculiar move on Maloney's part. Even though my retirement had been put off so that my case would stay alive, my security clearance had got an automatic suspension, as it does when the agent leaves active service but remains in reserve as I had. Maloney couldn't possibly have not known this, and so his action had to be mainly an expression of petty vengeance and face-saving, or possibly some sort of "warning" to me. Who knows? At this point, it was irrelevant.

By early 2004, I was getting tired of the nonaction on the part of the military re: my case. And not just nonaction—blatant, criminal obfuscation. The CID in Sacramento had contacted the CID in Iraq, who, in a moment of impressive though dispiriting candor, came right out and said they really didn't give a damn about torture, and not only were they not going to investigate, but they were going to actively cover it up (this was, of course, shortly before Abu Ghraib hit the headlines). So I decided to go to the FBI with my case. Guess who my report went to? You may have heard of him: James Comey.

Then, in early April 2004, a friend called me at work.

"You won't believe the pictures all over the news!" Abu Ghraib had broken upon the world, and nothing was ever the same for me or anyone else. Soon after, *60 Minutes*, which had been sitting on their story about torture at the prison, saw that other news outlets were covering it and decided to go ahead with their report. In short order, the *New Yorker* magazine published an exhaustive article by Seymour Hirsch about Abu Ghraib.

I thought of what the Egyptian lawyer back in Samarra had told me about the calculated release of horrendous images. It seemed as if somebody beat Halliburton to the punch—it would turn out that the source of the photos was not the giant corporation, but a regular guy from Maryland, Sgt. Joe Darby, an MP with the 372nd. He'd been at Abu Ghraib since October of 2003, had seen horrendous and horrible things, but had adapted. Later, he would describe himself as "no boy scout."

A fellow MP, Charles Graner, gave him a CD with sightseer-type photos on it, of places and scenes around Iraq. That wasn't all that was on the disc. Either Graner had included the torture photos intentionally, or he'd forgotten they were on there. Darby, the non-boy-scout, was sufficiently alarmed and disgusted by the now-famous images that he decided, after mulling it over for a couple of weeks, to put the CD in an envelope and slip it under the door of the CID. He said later that he never expected the worldwide uproar that followed. But the rest, as they say, is history. I wonder what Halliburton thought when Joe Darby, without their permission, stole their thunder . . .

Among the many dreadful images that flew around the world, one of the famously worst was that of a battered male corpse packed in ice while young American soldiers pose and cavort with the dead man, grinning and giving the "thumbs-up." It would turn out that the man, whose name was Manadel al-Jamadi, had died after a brief but lethal "interrogation" session during which his arms had been tied behind his back, and then he was hung up by his tightly bound wrists. In torture parlance, that's known as the "Strapaddo" position, and had been favored by the Spanish Inquisition.

There was a squabble between the CIA interrogators and the US military interrogators over whose fault the death was and who should cover up the truth and how they should do it. The CIA guys prevailed and skedaddled, leaving the MPs with the corpse and the problem.

Why was he packed in ice? To throw off, in the event of a post-mortem, the blood gas work that would be done, making it appear that he had died hours later than he had. And who came up with that idea? My sources tell me that it was none other than Col. Maloney, who was at Abu Ghraib on that day, as was Pappas, and that both had been in the room, watching, during the fatal interrogation. So they stashed the corpse in a shower room, iced him, and bought themselves some time while they scrambled to figure out a way to hide the truth from the other inmates. That was when the soldiers had their opportunity to pose for those fun pictures, and give him names like "Mr. Frosty." How would Maloney know about something as arcane as measuring blood gas in post-mortems? He'd been a sheriff in Marin County once upon a time. He'd have been privy to all that nasty business.

The next day, a fake IV was attached to the corpse and it was wheeled out. Col. Thomas Pappas was present for all of this, as he himself later testified, and was directly involved in the elaborately premeditated cover-up of the so-called "Ice Man's" torture and death in November of 2003. An autopsy would reveal that he died from asphyxiation. "I'm not going down for this alone," Pappas is quoted as saying at the time. In fact, he didn't go down at all; in 2007, he would be granted immunity in exchange for damning testimony in the court martial of one of his immediate subordinate officers. When I heard about this, I was not remotely surprised that he'd "flipped" on his officer.

How well I recalled Pappas's words, overheard by me behind the tents in Balad: "What the hell are we going to tell Karpinski?" And Maloney's reply: "Don't tell her anything."

Lie, conceal, cover up. That was the kind of men they were.

Pappas may not have gone down for it alone, but others did. A twenty-six-year-old American freelance radio-tower repairman named Nick Berg was about as alone as a man could be when he was beheaded by the then-leader of Al Qaeda in Iraq, Abu Musab al-Zarkawi, in early May 2004 after being kidnapped from a hotel in Baghdad about a month before—right around the time Abu Ghraib broke. There's a video of the beheading, and in it, one of the five masked fellows standing behind the condemned first reads a statement, making it clear that what they are about to do is retribution for Abu Ghraib. If my early warnings, and the warnings of others, had been heeded, and there had been a major change in the interrogation "culture," could Abu Ghraib, and all that followed, have been averted?

And it was retribution upon retribution. Zarkawi would be, for a couple of years, the leader of Al Qaeda in Iraq. He had an appetite for violence not just against Westerners, but against Shia Muslims, and here was his big opportunity. He was likely the planner of the bombing of the Golden Mosque at the Al Askari shrine in Samarra in early 2006, which set off waves of sectarian violence, and he bombed Shia shrines, set off car bombs and deployed suicide bombers elsewhere in Iraq, killing hundreds, if not thousands, of Shia Muslims. It got so bad that bin Laden himself is said to have sent a message to him telling him to cool it with the killing of other Muslims. Bad PR, he said. Zarkawi told bin Laden to go pound sand, that he'd do things his own way. In June of 2006, Zarkawi would die in a US air strike near Baqubah, Iraq, and al Baghdadi would ascend. We certainly kicked over the termite mound when we invaded that country. We were sent there to catch terrorists, the pretext being that Saddam harbored Al Qaeda. We ended up plowing the ground and fertilizing it for the hearty growth of Al Qaeda in Iraq, which morphed into ISIS. Not unlike strains of bacteria morphing into ever more deadly and antibiotic-resistant forms.

In the aftermath of the breaking story of Abu Ghraib, the news people got wind of me and my case. Soon there were TV trucks on the lawn and constant phone calls. There were countless news releases, to the point where the California National Guard got extremely antsy at all the unwanted attention, and whined to me about it. I was only too happy to remind them of the tangled web they'd woven.

"Hey, you said I was crazy, remember? I can't be held accountable if I'm crazy," I said to Col. Quentin. "And if I'm not crazy, and you knew it, and renditioned me out of the country without orders, then what does that mean?" Quentin bridled at this.

"We don't want to hear that word 'rendition,'" he said.

"Oh, okay," I said. "Then how about abduction? Or maybe kidnapping? You like those words better?"

Meanwhile, I watched incredulously as everyone named in my case got promoted: Maloney, for instance, was made an IG for the National Guard. Segura got promoted to Major, and made into an Intelligence Officer for the National Guard. Later, both would get plum jobs with Booz-Allen, a giant "management and information technology consulting firm" in McLean, VA. Neither, in my opinion, had the slightest qualification for such exalted positions. More of my opinion—these cushy sinecures were their "reward" for keeping a tight lid on inconvenient facts about WMD, about torture, and about the whole sorry business.

Remember that first top-secret briefing at the 223rd headquarters, when we were about to learn that we'd be going to Iraq? I mentioned a warrant officer present at that briefing, and that he was Kathy's cousin. This fellow was on staff at Abu Ghraib. He would tell me, right around the time Maloney, Segura, and Pappas were getting their "rewards," that he'd heard them say more than once that they weren't going to let Ford get between them and the six-figure salaries they had in their sights.

Pappas would eventually be "disciplined" for his role in Abu Ghraib with a four hundred dollar fine, in addition to the immunity he got for his testimony against a subordinate, and then given a good job at Langley, as head of the spy school there. Much later, I'd learn that Pappas had had a mental breakdown right around the time of Abu Ghraib and was transferred to Germany, but was promoted and reinstated anyway.

And I discovered how Maloney was using his new "powers:" Acting on a hunch, I went to the IG office in Sacramento and discovered that all of my records—medical records, service records—were gone, vanished. I confronted an officer, demanding to know if Maloney was behind it. The officer dissembled.

"We can do anything we want," he said. So true.

At about this same time, I found out that May, my former "teammate" in Samarra, had been giving interviews, shooting her mouth off about how, contrary to world opinion and contrary to my repeated warnings, the US military needed to actually get "tougher" with the Iraqis. I also learned that Maloney and the others swiftly moved to put a "gag" on her.

Also around this time, videos of torture at Samarra surfaced, filmed by Pete Fischer, the same guy who filmed the destruction of the VX gas canisters in Balad. The CID mentioned the torture videos to me, seeming to not realize that the videos corroborated my charges.

What, I wondered, could be going through their minds? Soon after, I got a call that caused me to further question the brains, sense, and sanity of the CID people I was dealing with:

"We're getting all these reports out of Samarra," said the officer. "Why didn't you say something sooner?" It was a forehead-slapping moment.

"I beg your pardon," I said. "I'm the guy who was strapped to the stretcher and kidnapped for reporting this stuff long before Abu Ghraib, remember?" He backpedaled quickly.

"Oh, right, of course."

I could only shake my head in wonder. And I thought I was with the Keystone Cops when I was in Iraq . . . .

———————

Before Abu Ghraib broke, my aim had been to file my case in civilian court. So far, all my filings had been within the military and the government—the IG, the CID, the FBI—and had been demands for official investigation. Now, with Abu Ghraib's lurid images seared onto the consciousness of the world and the ugly truth laid bare, there was an immediate Iraqi backlash. Americans taken prisoner in Iraq were subjected to escalating retaliation: beatings, beheadings, and other brutal treatment. Conscious of the well-being of the troops on the ground and the further inflammatory effect my case might have for them if it were to enter the civilian sphere in the form of a trial, I made the tough decision to hold off, to not take the next step of bringing my case to the civilian courts, where I might actually see some action, until the war was officially over.

Little did I suspect, in 2004, how many long years I would have to wait . . .

And here's a curious little note. Remember our old pal Mahmoud? Remember what I said about my suspicions that he was using his chumminess with our intel unit in Iraq to further some exotic agenda of his own in the post-Saddam chaos? Right around this time, when Abu Ghraib was breaking, I got a call from the FBI, saying they needed my "help." They asked me to come in and look at some photos to assist them in identifying an Iraqi operative involved in a possible conspiracy to reinstate the monarchy in Iraq, which ended in 1958 with the execution of Faisal II during the July Revolution. The king was dead, but there were surviving far-flung cousins. Here was their chance to get back on the throne, and this operative was apparently assisting.

The FBI showed me pictures of several men, like a lineup. A couple of them I didn't recognize at all, but one of them was as familiar as my own face in the mirror: Mahmoud. Nothing ever came of it, but I felt vindicated.

I could only imagine the position Mahmoud envisioned for himself in the resurrected royal house of Iraq . . .

# CHAPTER 27

# CROCODILE TEARS

"Do you know this person?" The photo was of an elderly, unshaven, dirty, bruised, unhappy (but living) man.

"Yes," I said. "I know this man. Very well."

The two CID guys looked at me intently. "Tell us what you know."

I laughed bitterly. "You don't want to ask me about this."

But they were adamant. "We have to. There's some serious investigation going on."

"Okay," I sighed. "This man is Abu Seger, also known as Ali Sa'ad Hasaan. He was Saddam's banker." Looks of astonishment registered on the two guys' faces.

And I told them about the raid on Seger's house, the mountain of cash, the arrest, the vital intel I got from him, the transport to Tikrit, and the subsequent transport to Abu Ghraib.

Earlier that morning, I'd just arrived to start my day at Folsom, when another corrections officer ran over to me.

"There are a couple of guys here who want to talk to you!"

I was exasperated. *Now what?*

The guys were from the CID. We adjourned to a side room. That was when they showed me the picture of Abu Seger. My heart dropped at the sight of his face. I'd done pretty well encasing my sorrow and regret over this man in a hard protective shell, but it cracked for a moment.

"How did he die?" one of the men asked.

By now I was well past any decorum.

"You tell me," I shot back.

They gave me a cock-and-bull story about Abu Seger dying in a mortar attack in the prison yard. I just looked at them.

"Oh, knock it off, will you? Jesus Christ, I've had it with you guys."

They were taken aback, but they asked for the truth. I gave them the rest of the details: about the torture of Abu Seger, starting in Samarra with Stavros braining him with an iron rod rolled into a newspaper, and the torture culminating with me seeing, with my own eyes, Seger dying on the gurney at Abu Ghraib from what was obviously a beating administered by human hands. Because these guys were writing down everything I said, I gave them a graphic description of the contre-coup and the terrible breathing, just for good measure. I got perverse enjoyment out of watching them scramble to keep up and not leave out any details. When I was done, they said:

"We need you to come in and make a statement."

Again, I just looked at them as if they were perhaps a little slow.

"My case, which I'm sure you're familiar with, includes the abuse, torture, and death of this incredibly valuable and high-profile asset. And you surely know I'm now talking to the FBI about this, right? I'm talking to the FBI because I'm tired of my case going nowhere with the military."

They hemmed and hawed. The meeting wasn't going as planned. It was obvious that they'd come here hoping I'd corroborate the phony mortar attack story. Either they weren't familiar with my case, or they thought maybe I was ready to change my story. They quickly understood that they were on a fool's errand, though. I could see, by their faces and body language, the moment when they decided not to press their suit, so to speak. They didn't leave me empty-handed, though I'd have been happy to go the rest of my life innocent of the piece of knowledge they imparted to me before they left.

It was from these guys that I learned of the tall baseball-cap-wearing Anglo pulling up in an American sedan in front of the field hospital in Balad, opening the trunk, and in broad daylight, hoisting out a battered corpse, dumping it on the steps, getting back in his car, and driving away.

That corpse was Abu Seger.

In a follow-up contact with these same guys, I learned that Stavros, whose name was prominent in the info I gave them during the Folsom visit, was in "therapy" in Boston for the "trauma" he'd suffered by being named in my case. The CID guys gave me a look, as if to say: And it's your fault poor Stavros is suffering so. *This*, I thought, *takes the almighty cake . . .*

Soon after the visit at Folsom from the CID guys with their bogus story about Abu Seger's death, attacks on my veracity started to appear online from a group called VeriSEAL, whose stated mission is to ferret out and expose anyone trying to fake being a Navy SEAL. The man making the attacks was one Lenny Masters (not his real name) from the CIA's attachment to the State Department. His brand name should be Hoaxes 'r' Us. This was the same guy who, a few years later, would spread a made-up story about an anti-white tirade by Michelle Obama, had tried to frame John Kerry with war crimes from the Vietnam Era via doctored interview audios, and who would spread a totally fake rumor about British intelligence wiretapping Trump in 2016.

But Masters himself was not the initiator of the VeriSEAL attacks; I would learn that the string-puller behind Masters was none other than Hector Segura. What they did was simple but effective; they posted a Photoshopped picture on the VeriSEAL site showing me with a Navy Seal Trident pinned to my uniform. I'd never claimed to be a Navy SEAL; what I'd said, truthfully, was that thirty years before I'd been a corpsman attached to the Navy Seals as a medic. Big difference. When I heard that Segura had employed Masters to be his front man, I could easily believe it. CHIMS (Combined Human Intelligence Management System)—the complex computerized tool we used in Iraq for every intelligence purpose you can imagine— included advanced Photoshopping. And who had intimate knowledge of CHIMS, and access? Segura, of course.

Next, a book came to my attention, recounting, among other incidents, Abu Seger's death. I hurled the book into the river when I got to the part where a doctor expressed his "expert" opinion that the medic—and he named me here—present when Abu Seger was being interrogated in Samarra was equally to blame for Seger's ultimate injuries and death. Boiling with fury, I tracked the doc down at some back east hospital and confronted him via telephone. The guy dissembled feebly before saying he was on duty and hung up.

I followed up with a letter demanding a retraction; the guy responded, protesting that it wasn't his fault, that the material he read was heavily redacted, and that this was the conclusion he drew. I blasted him:

"And you let this completely false, libelous statement be published without even fact-checking or consulting me? How hard would it have been to pick up the phone? Are you lazy *and* greedy?"

But this was just one guy, and hardly the worst lie that would be told. The blame-and-defame game was well underway.

Though as word of my story got out there more and more, the reaction was not always fiction and distortion.

In 2004, Helmar Buechel, a dynamic reporter for the international German news magazine Der Spiegel, contacted me and came to Sacramento to interview me in person, sympathetically, as part of a series on Americans committing atrocities in Iraq. Buechel heard my story—it must have been the thousandth time I'd told it—and was particularly astonished when I got to the part about the drugging and kidnapping.

Buechel, who personified the term "go-getter," tracked my old friend Dr. Pia Navarro to her home in southern California. She was out of the military and in private practice by then, nearly incognito, hair dyed, and with a virtual firewall around her. She certainly had not given any interviews nor made any public statements or appearances. Buechel and his crew lay in wait, just like in the movies, inside nondescript cars and vans parked on her street. They took her totally by surprise, ambushing her when she arrived home from work, leaping forth with cameras, lights, and microphones.

Buechel confronted her aggressively:

"Dr. Navarro, what did you do in Iraq? What did you do to Agent Gregory Ford? Is it true that you aided and abetted his kidnapping after he came to you for help?"

With neighbors watching and her flummoxed husband standing in the door of their house, Navarro backed away from Buechel, offering self-exculpatory words which, when I heard them, impressed me with their bold audacity:

"He's my patient," she said, looking like the proverbial deer in the headlights. "I can't tell you anything about this without a written statement from him!"

And she ducked inside and slammed the door. Later, Buechel showed the footage to me so I could confirm Navarro's identity. And Buechel was thorough; he also had photos of the rest of the motley crew for me to ID: Maloney, Segura, Pappas, Stavros, May, and Richter. The Navarro/Ford footage became part of a three-part documentary which showed in Germany and got, so I heard, record-breaking viewership.

Perhaps because of this publicity and because of Abu Ghraib, a heavily redacted memo by the CID surfaced in mid-2004, confirming that Navarro's commanders ordered her to drug and interrogate me.

Later in 2004, a guy I knew named Dave Debatto, a journalist and counter-intelligence agent who served in Iraq at the same time I did, interviewed me and published an article in Salon titled "Whitewashing Torture." Maloney, Segura, and Navarro all ignored requests by DeBatto to be interviewed for the story. In the article, Debatto also briefly recounted the stories of other whistle-blowers who were locked up, demoted, libeled, harassed, and discredited in response to their reports of abuse, torture, and gross misconduct.

In 2005, DeBatto interviewed Janis Karpinski (who had been demoted to Colonel in the aftermath of Abu Ghraib). In that interview, she made it clear that the orders to employ certain torture techniques came from way, way above. She named Rumsfeld himself as authorizing private contractors to use these illegal torture methods on prisoners and to "educate" the young MPs at the prison in the torture arts. She also said that Col. Geoffrey "Ghitmo-ize Abu Ghraib" Miller, who replaced her after her suspension from duty following the outbreak of the scandal, had told her, before the shit hit the fan, that you had to treat prisoners "like dogs" or else lose control of them. She said she'd been kept in the dark and had been scapegoated. I might not have readily believed this if I hadn't overheard Maloney and Pappas's little between-the-tents tête-à-tête. I wanted very much to get an introduction to Karpinski, to talk to her, to tell her about my case and what I'd heard and to hear her side of the story. I asked Dave for her phone number. He never said he wouldn't give it to me, but he managed to postpone and forget and put off until he and I lost touch. That was a major disappointment.

In 2005, Lynddie England and her compatriots—fall guys, I knew, for their command and on up the chain of authority to the highest levels of government—went on trial for Abu Ghraib atrocities. Unlike Stavros, May, and Richter, named as abusers and torturers in my case, who, knowing about official post-9/11 relaxations on the definition of torture, had acted on their own volition (except maybe for some encouragement from Mahmoud), England and the others going on trial had received direct orders from above to perpetrate the terrorizing and sexual humiliation of prisoners. It's a crucial difference. I wanted very much to testify in court on their behalf.

You ask why? There were major differences between my Samarra "team" and England and her cohort. The Samarra people were anything but high school dropout types. None of them had ever worked in a chicken-processing plant before signing up, as England had. They were all college-educated, some— Richter and Stavros most notably—holding advanced degrees and speaking numerous languages. I wasn't happy about this up-close and personal demonstration that rigorous education is no deterrent to atavistic behavior. It belied the common prejudice that lack of education makes humans more prone to violence. We'd have to look deeper and harder for the sources of brutishness, beyond our knee-jerk biases. And I, a believer in education as our best hope for improving the species, was deeply disturbed by the ominous implication: that being "educated" (and therefore confident and entitled) might actually bring out the worst in violence-prone individuals.

I recalled the reaction of my "team" when I warned them that their methods were severely pissing off the Iraqis, putting us all in danger.

Instead of taking heed, Stavros in particular seemed to take it as a direct challenge and became even more aggressive and sadistic. And the ones who had the power to order Stavros, Richter, and May to quit—Maloney, Segura, and Pappas—did not.

My bet was that if Lynddie England et al—way less ambitious than the Samarra gang and unburdened by the latter's sense of privilege and entitlement—had been similarly warned, they'd have desisted. They did what they were ordered to do, and those orders came down from Bush, Cheney, Rumsfeld, and the rest of the gang. Unsophisticated, easily dissed, and publicly denigrated as ignoramuses and white trash and such, called "bad apples" by G. W. Bush, they were the perfect scapegoats. In military lingo, they were the "recycled hillbillies" who made up so much of the vast army of expendables, sent out there to do the dirty work and sometimes die in this corrupt war. In her public statements, Karpinski had made it plain that she thought of this the same way I did—that she didn't believe that these youthful MPs had the confidence or arrogance to think up these shenanigans on their own.

My feelings about this were so strong that I added to the terms of settlement in my case that if I prevailed, England and the others would be pardoned and Janis Karpinski's rank would either be restored or she'd be promoted. There was no doubt in my mind that Pappas's dereliction in reporting abuse and torture both in Samarra and at Abu Ghraib to Gen. Karpinski, Pappas's boss, was a deliberate setup of Karpinski. Again, that conversation I overheard in Balad between Maloney and Pappas about what to tell Karpinski was, for me, direct proof. How I wished I could confer with her directly about all of this!

Around the time of the trial of Lynddie England et al, I was contacted by the CID. I told them of my desire to testify.

"Have you been called to testify?" they asked.

"No, I haven't."

"Well, then you can't go," they said. "And if you do go, we'll make sure you don't get through the door."

"But *you* could call me to testify," I said. "You know that I know what really happened."

The CID's reaction to that suggestion was the usual: dissembling, throat-clearing, and foot-shuffling.

"Uh, we'll get back to you." I'd expected no less. And I thought: *When you're railroading someone into the hoosegow, the last thing you want is countermanding evidence.* The same CID guys call me a few days later, saying:

"Oh, we just wanted to make sure you're still in Sacramento."

And I thought: *Not too obvious or anything.* Plainly, they were nervous that I might fly in unannounced and make a surprise appearance in the courtroom. And I would learn that the local IG, Evan Holmes (not his real name), had contacted the CID in Washington and specifically told them NOT to bring me in to testify, to keep me out of that courtroom no matter what.

Later still, I'd learn that Janis Karpinski also wanted to testify on behalf of the accused, and was similarly not invited.

---

During the time of the trial of England and the others, it became more and more evident that the IG people were looking for any excuse they could find to drop my case and halt any investigation, and that they were in fact downright hostile to me and my case. Evan Holmes and a sidekick paid a special visit to the office of the Adjutant General of the National Guard just a few blocks from my home in Sacramento.

I met them there, along with Kevin Healey. Holmes and his pal were armed with angles and arguments they plainly hoped would lead to the collapse of my charges. And let me tell you, they were really reaching for the sky.

They tried to say, for instance, that since I was not a pharmacological neurologist, how could I possibly know that I was given mind-altering drugs?—hoping, obviously, to make me back down. When Kevin Healey informed them that he was going to record the entire encounter, Holmes tried to say that was illegal. Healey knew it was not.

"I'm a Judge Advocate General, remember?" he reminded Holmes. "I know the law around here."

But Holmes still wouldn't back down, and the encounter got intense. Healey knew that this was a high-stakes game of chicken, and that the slightest sign of weakness or hesitation could be fatal. He met Holmes head-to-head. They were like a couple of battling grizzlies, each trying to out-roar the other. Holmes eventually stormed out of the office, shouting:

"You'll have my report!"

In September 2005, a few days before that report arrived, a source in D. C. called, asked about my case and whether I'd heard anything yet, then dropped a bombshell; the head of the IG, Joseph Schmitz, who put his stamp of approval or disapproval on every investigation, had just resigned under pressure, accused of trashing, at the behest of Donald Rumsfeld, any investigations pertaining to war crimes, anything at all that would show the Department of the Army in a bad light. Schmitz was plainly falling on his sword for Rumsfeld.

But it seems as if Schmitz got in at least one last lick. When the report arrived from IG Holmes following the meeting at the Sacramento National Guard office, it declared, with no mention anywhere of the fact that JAG attorney Healy was present at that meeting: *We find no credibility to Ford's case.*

In 2005, Democratic California Congressman Henry Waxman led an investigation into waste and fraud and vast quantities of missing cash in Iraq starting in 2003. Many shipments of staggering sums, billions and trillions of dollars, went in and out of the country on big C-130 military transport planes in an operation known as the Green Zone Cyprus Express, the money—both incoming and outgoing—never accounted for. Waxman's probe reveals a specific load in the amount of $750 million being added to an outbound shipment to the island of Cyprus (where money was regularly unloaded and never seen again) not long after the raid on Abu Seger's house.

Meanwhile, the Iraq war dragged on and on, and my case languished. At the end of December 2011, the war was declared "officially" over, and I was free, at long last, to file in civilian court. The first court I filed with was the 6th District Court in Sacramento. Not only did I file against the original gang of perps— Maloney, Segura, Pappas, May, Stavros, and Richter—but I also put in a claim for my rightful percentage of the $750 million seized in the raid on Abu Seger's house.

The response was discouraging. Not only did the 6th District Court rule that they didn't have the power to deal with war crimes and false imprisonment, but Maloney and Segura, in their "answer" to the charges, simply stuck to their story: no WMD discovered, no torture or abuse, and no $750 million seized in Samarra.

From 2011 on, the case got kicked upstairs multiple times—from the 6th District Court to the 9th Circuit Court and then on up through different levels of the 9th, and eventually, all the way to the docket of the Supreme Court of the United States.

# CHAPTER 28

# THE TELLTALE HEART

I watched the face of the VA (Veterans' Affairs) doctor while he moved a stethoscope around on my chest. It was like watching someone listen to a news report of a plane crash or a tsunami. His brows knitted together, then shot up in astonishment, then knitted together again while he looked down in concentration. Then he pulled the earpieces out and put a hand on my shoulder.

"Stay right here. Don't move. I'm calling the emergency room to come and get you."

It was now 2011. As the years went by since my return from Iraq, my health had deteriorated. I'd experienced gradually worsening symptoms that included breathing problems, a persistent cough, heart problems, and fluid in my lungs.

One really alarming symptom I'd noticed was chunks of memory missing. One memory, though, was strong, persistent, unvarying, and unwavering: being on the plane, strapped down, mysterious liquid entering my vein through an IV, paralysis snaking along my limbs and then faces leaning over me, voices pressing me with questions. A conviction grew that whatever drug had been used, it was more than merely consciousness-altering; it was some sort of MK Ultra (CIA-sanctioned mind-control experiments conducted from the fifties to the seventies) drug they'd pumped into me.

My health problems were becoming acute.

So far, the VA, though it had made efforts to treat me, had not been overly helpful in regard to my theory that an exotic illegal drug was used on me. Their attitude was: "The US military wouldn't do that kind of thing!"

I persisted, though, and soon connected with Dr. Detloffsen, a former Navy MD, lieutenant commander and also a SEAL, who'd come out of retirement and gone to work at the VA. It so happened that this doc had a major interest in nerve gas and burn-pit issues and such. He's a neurologist, with a specialty in neuropsychopharmacology. This guy and I made friends pretty quickly. Looking at my record, he saw what was there about rendition and drugging. He came keenly to attention.

"Tell me about this," he said, looking at me intently.

I described the drugging on the plane and what I'd experienced in as much detail as I could muster. He paid close attention and did not look as if he was just being polite while secretly thinking: *This guy's nuts.* And then he spoke:

"Everything you're describing sounds like a certain specific outlawed drug made for the MK Ultra program. It's a perfect match. I ought to know. I was with the MK Ultra research team."

I was gob smacked. Mind you, I had not mentioned my suspicion about a secret drug, only my experience and symptoms.

"And what's the name of this drug?" I asked, hardly daring to hear it articulated, like speaking an incantation that might summon a demon.

"Sodium amytal," said the doctor. "Its long-term effects perfectly match your ongoing symptoms. Let me listen to your heart."

And he put the stethoscope to my chest.

When he said he was calling the emergency room to come and get me, I naturally asked what was up.

"You have A-fib," he said, picking up the phone, "and I'm betting it was caused by the application of sodium amytal. That's one of the long-term effects of that drug."

———————

I was whisked off to the ICU, where they found fluid on one lung and where they defibrillated me. Soon after, I asked the doctor if he'd help with my case.

"No problem at all," he said. "I will sign any document at all stating that in my opinion that's what caused your conditions: memory, breathing, and especially, heart."

A little later, I went in for a procedure known as ablation, where they snake a device up your femoral artery and into your heart, to permanently eliminate the A-fib, which I had never had before the drugging on the plane.

And who specifically ordered up this cocktail of misery?

It was already known that Capt. Pia Navarro, MD, received orders from Maloney and Segura to rendition me, drug me, and interrogate me. What was not known was the name of the drug that was used. As a trained intelligence agent, I was highly resistant to interrogation under the influence of more common drugs such as sodium pentothal. Maloney and Segura—and quite likely somebody else way higher up the food chain (I suspect Rumsfeld himself)—knew this, and ordered the use of the one MK Ultra drug known to possibly work on such trained agents: sodium amytal. Navarro surely understood the dangers of this drug, but she gave it to me anyway. Doubtless she also understood the possible long-term effects, including brain damage; I couldn't help but wonder if eventual brain damage and memory loss were exactly what they were hoping for.

It's likely that she received those orders during the layover in Kuwait, when she left the room where I was resting, leaving behind her medical report. I recalled the change in her manner between the time she left the room, still relatively friendly and talkative, and how she was when she returned: grim-faced, cold, and uncommunicative. Navarro was named in the initial post-rendition charges, but when I learned what dangerous, highly illegal drug I was likely given on the plane, I added that to the charges against her. I would eventually learn that the last surviving copy of the orders she received in Kuwait was locked away in a safety-deposit box by Navarro and her sidekick on the flight, Jon Weber.

And what was it that was so crucial for them to know that this drug was pumped into me on the plane? What were those faces leaning over me asking about? Why were they probing, using those enigmatic words *Copper Green*?

In short, Copper Green is a code name for a US and global "black ops" program sanctioned by Rumsfeld, starting with the 2001 invasion of Afghanistan. It essentially gives license to "grab whoever you must, do whatever you want."

Its techniques of torture and coercion were geared and custom-tailored toward Arab men, and included, as I mentioned before, culture-specific methods of shame, terror, and sexual humiliation designed to elicit information. Abu Ghraib, as the world would soon learn from the photos, was ground zero for the application of these techniques. Earlier experiments had been carried out during Gulf War 1, as I'd learned from that Egyptian lawyer back in Samarra. Abu Ghraib was, among other things, something of a "laboratory" for Copper Green, where the "bugs" of these methods and techniques could be worked out on the captive subjects.

By the time I was on that plane, my vociferous objections to torture and abuse were well known, and it would appear that my interrogators wanted to know what I knew about the top secret Copper Green and who I might have spoken to about it. I did in fact know about Copper Green, but I surmised that while I was under the influence of sodium amytal, I did not spill any beans. If I had, my bet is that I would likely not still be alive. The fact that Lynddie England and the others, all of them just poorly educated enlisted folk, were employing specific Copper Green methods was proof to me that their orders had come from above—way, way above.

And I know all too bitterly well that the best remedy for such secret operations is a good dose of the light of day. If my repeated warnings about the torture going on in Samarra had been listened to, and taken seriously, the investigation would have extended to Abu Ghraib much sooner, and a lot of grief—including the world-wide scandal itself and country-wide anti-American insurgency in Iraq—might have been prevented.

———

The eyes of the store proprietor were magnified almost comically by her jeweler's glasses when she looked up from her work to greet me as I stepped into her shop.

It was a perfect cloudless day on the northern California coast. Such days are just rare enough there that when they happen, it's hard not to feel blessed and ebullient. I've seen more of this planet than most people have, and let me tell you, that coastline rivals, in sheer wild beauty, any place in the world.

The year was 2013, and fed up with the way my case seemed to be permanently stuck in the bureaucratic mud, I'd decided to go to the Fort Bragg (California, not North Carolina) office of Congressman Mike Thompson to see if I could interest him in shaking things up. He wasn't there, but his assistant was, and she promised to convey the details of my story to Thompson. That would also turn out to be a dead end, but the trip was scarcely a waste of time. Heading back on Highway One, we pulled into Mendocino, nine miles south of Fort Bragg, to stroll around, peek into shops and have some lunch.

It was certainly not my first visit—I'd been coming to Mendocino for years from my home further down the coast. I once had family connections there, plus I can confidently claim it's one of the top ten most beautiful places on the planet. Somebody once said about Mendocino that it looks like the little toy town a model train circles around, only quite real and human-scaled and perched on a promontory of high rugged cliffs over the mighty Pacific.

Even if you've never been there, you've probably seen Mendocino, though you may not have realized it. It's been the setting for countless movies, like *The Russians Are Coming, The Russians Are Coming!*, *East of Eden*, *Racing with the Moon*, and many, many more. If you ever watched the TV series *Murder, She Wrote*, set in the fictional New England town of Cabot Cove, you've seen Mendocino.

There was a *Twilight Zone* episode years ago where a man gets on a commuter train, falls asleep, travels for a while, wakes up, and when the train stops, he's in an idyllic 1880s village. That *TZ* episode was not filmed in Mendocino, but it could have been. I always thought of it whenever I went there. You often hear the word "magic" when people rhapsodize about Mendocino.

When we stopped for lunch that day, we spied an attractive little jewelry shop, stepped in for a look, and got into a conversation with the proprietor. It was a surreal moment: that was when she looked up and greeted me with magnified eyes.

She soon raised her jeweler's glasses and engaged me in pleasant conversation. She asked what brought us to town. I told her I was on my way back from

Thompson's office, told her a little about my case and mentioned that I had been in Iraq in 2003.

"Oh," said the proprietor. "My cousin was in Iraq, then, too."

I asked the cousin's name, on the remote off-chance that it might be one I recognized. I was expecting her to say Joe Blow or Bill Jones or something along those lines.

Her answer redefined the overworked expression "jaw-dropping." Mine fell to the floor like an ore bucket. I think I might have stolen a glance outside, looking for Rod Serling leaning against a lamppost.

"Her name's Janis Karpinski."

What were we saying about Mendocino magic? It was one of those moments of serendipity that makes a person contemplate the mechanics of fate. A tiny little window of chance opens, you pass through, and everything changes forever. Through this connection, General Karpinski and I met over the phone, became great friends, exchanged hours and hours of conversation about my experiences, hers, the critical overlap of the two, and each of us learned crucial and heretofore unknown facts that affected our respective cases.

One of the first things I told her about was the what'll-we-tell-Karpinski conversation I overheard in Balad, earwitness proof that her second in command, Col. Pappas, was willing to premeditatedly keep her in the dark. If he was willing to do that, it was with the likely intention of setting her up to take the fall if his own gross dereliction ever came to light.

She asked me to tell her, to the best of my ability, exactly when and where this overheard conversation had taken place. I said it had been in the last week of June 2003, in Balad, just before I was rudely removed.

She was astonished, but not surprised. She said it all rang true, that she had heard bits and pieces, knew something was going on with an intel agent in Samarra reporting torture, but never got the whole picture. The timing of that overheard conversation fit perfectly, she said, with the timing of fragments of information that had come to her attention. I told her that I had tried to get my reports of torture and abuse to her; she said she never got them. This was exactly what I thought would happen, that Maloney, Segura, and Pappas would purposely obstruct and obfuscate.

There was a long silence on the other end of the phone as she digested all of this.

"Uncontrollable," she finally said. "They were completely out of control."

And she corroborated Henry Waxman's findings about the likely fate of the vanished $750 million and my 20 percent of it.

"I know exactly where your money went," she said. "One day in the Green Zone in Baghdad, something caught my eye: an unscheduled C-130 sitting on the runway."

Karpinski and her entourage had gone over and asked the crew who they were and what they were doing.

"This is the money run," they said. "We're taking a load to Cyprus." And they showed her paperwork, signed by Paul Bremer, authorizing the run. She had no reason to think it was not all on the up-and-up, and let them go. She had no way of knowing that from Cyprus, that money would disappear into various private accounts and never be mentioned again. The guys on the tarmac had, it seemed, readily 'fessed up, thinking they were "busted," and had surely been surprised when she let them go.

We compared notes on the timing of this, too; this incident occurred shortly after the raid on Abu Seger's house.

Maloney and Segura knew the money would never have been found if not for me and the intel I got from the Sheik, and that I was entitled to that percentage, though, as I mentioned earlier, I didn't know it at the time. I had not gone into Abu Seger's house, nor watched the money being counted, with an expectation of a reward. How well I remember, though, the two of them popping up in Samarra in the immediate aftermath of the seizure and subsequent disappearance, giving me the fish eye. Knowing what I know now, it's obvious what they were thinking: How could they get around paying me, and how could they keep a chunk of it for themselves? One way would be to have me declared insane. Meaning that well before I filed charges of abuse and torture, the wheels were probably already turning to discredit me (starting with the cover-up of the WMD in Balad) by portraying me as "mentally unstable." I believe that this is why they never responded to any of my intel reports, because to do so would undermine the picture they wanted to paint—that I was crazy. Also years later, I would come across a memo passed between Maloney and Segura soon after I'd been shipped out of Iraq. That memo would become the opening statement of my lawsuit.

In 2017, the Supreme Court would decide not to hear the case, because, they said, of the flood of other war crimes cases it would precipitate. My lawyer, Mick Harrison, and I are undaunted, and intend to appeal. The case is still on the Supreme Court docket. And thanks to the ripple of fate that put me in that little shop in that little town on the northern California coast one fine day, I now have a powerful witness and ally in my case: Janis Karpinski, who submitted to the court a strong letter of support for me. She has a case of her own against the CIA, and her lawyers and mine are in close touch. We have every intention of moving forward.

The fifty-two medical reports I shipped home from Balad right before I was strapped to the gurney are stashed away and await their day in court, along with a pile of other damning documents. With them is another valuable souvenir: the Carlyle bill of lading showing the American provenance of the WMD, the discovery of which was simply denied.

And what were the words passed between Maloney and Segura, the first words any court that hears the case will read?

*We've got the whistle-blower safely locked up in the nut house. Now we can get back to raping and pillaging.*

# CUI BONO?

I did finish medical school, by the way.

In 2005-2006, I resumed my studies and graduated. But I didn't go on to practice medicine. I felt too damaged, too angry. The corrosive memories I carried of what I saw in Iraq, plus bitterness over the outrageous responses (and non-responses) to my reports of what I'd seen and experienced, the lies, obfuscation and arrogance, made me, I thought, temperamentally unsuited to be a healer. And I believed I had lost my "edge," thanks to the drugging on the plane. I had an unnervingly clear vision of myself lapsing into incompetence, turning into one of those seedy old MDs whose livelihood is his prescription pad.

By the year 2006, when I graduated, the opioid epidemic currently ravaging the United States was on a steep rise, the number of deaths per year already alarming, just about half way to what it is today. We tend to think of the epidemic as mainly afflicting the white population, and indeed that's true, but what you don't hear much about is the way it's tearing Native American families and lives apart, from the lower forty-eight to Canada to Alaska. The death rate in these communities—the Cherokee included—is easily as high as the death rate among whites. I had an ominous fear of a perverse future where I was part of this destruction, where I gradually and insidiously became an agent of harm.

And so I put my medical degree on the shelf. This was just one of the losses, along with my heart disorders, that I squarely attribute to the sodium amytal, the gift that keeps on giving.

Not long after medical school and the painful decision not to practice, I consoled myself with some traveling, including a trip to Sikkim in northern India and a visit to a monastery high, high in the Himalayas. On the way to the monastery, we passed a village with the actual name of Shambhala. As if that weren't enough, I was soon in the great hall of the monastery, brilliantly painted angels and demons swarming on the walls in the flicker of a thousand butter lamps, gazing upon a gold Buddha at least twenty feet high while monks blew the giant *dungchen* horns.

There's a legend in Buddhism of a saint named Issa (EYE-sa), rumored to be Jesus himself; it's said that he traveled from Jerusalem to the high mountains of northern India and spent time in Buddhist monasteries there, studying and teaching. The lama of the monastery I visited that day asked if I would like to see a portrait of Issa, drawn, so he said, from life. I said yes, of course, are you kidding? He reached way high up with a long, long pole to a glass-fronted cub-byhole adjacent to the gold Buddha, opened the glass door and brought down an ancient yak-leather bound parchment. The portrait had been rendered in charcoal. The face was a familiar one: Issa, whoever he was, had a distinctly Middle Eastern look about him.

In that moment, in that setting, confronted with such compelling mystery, I felt the grinding concerns that had been consuming me—lawsuits, lies, bitter disappointments, betrayals, and setbacks—receding, at least temporarily.

In March of 2018, I had a cerebral hemorrhage. I was comatose for weeks, trapped in a world of delirium and frightening visions. Here's just one: remember the giant desert lizards I saw in Iraq standing next to the road on their hind legs, watching us after we left Baghdad? They reappeared in my hallucinations, only now they were fourteen feet tall and pitted against puny little helpless human gladiators in a nightmare coliseum, complete with roaring crowd. It was utterly real, with smells, dust, hot sun, and blood, and I was trapped, unable to wake up.

People who saw me while I was in the hospital tell me now they thought I was a goner. When I first started to wake up, it was only halfway, and the under-worldly visions clung to my struggling consciousness as I tried to emerge. I'm told that my speech was garbled and raving, that I fought the doctors and nurses, and pulled out IVs. My family and friends were facing the possibility that I'd be a ruin in a wheelchair with a permanently fractured mind. Was this another effect of the drug pumped into me when I was renditioned? That's what I believe.

But I recovered. Within months, after a lot of hard, hard work and with the calm, resolute support of Kathy, without whom I could very well have wound up in that wheelchair watching cartoons in a day room somewhere, I got back on my feet, and my brain cleared and reengaged with my tongue in a way that seems miraculous to me and everyone around me.

Then, in September of 2018, we were in a parking lot in a little town south of Mendocino, Kathy at the wheel because I didn't feel I was quite ready to drive a car safely. We were waiting for a parking spot to open up, not moving, when *wham!* we got T-boned, hard, on the driver's side toward the rear of the car, by somebody backing out of another space.

Damn, I thought; this is a nuisance, but nobody seems to be hurt. Hardly a huge deal. A fender-bender. I got out to have a look at the damage and to talk to the driver of the other car, get insurance info and the rest of it. By the time I got to the driver's window, I was shaking as if I were being electrocuted, and could hardly speak, waves of adrenaline coming out of nowhere, my body spasming, and my back seizing up. You'd think I'd just been in a mortar attack in Samarra or something.

In fact, that's what my nervous system believed. It was classic, full-on PTSD. We went to a nearby clinic. This California coast seems to be the Zone of Coincidence; the physician's assistant who treated me in this itty-bitty little town was a woman who'd worked in Afghanistan for several years, specifically treating soldiers suffering from PTSD after combat with the Taliban. She recognized the symptoms instantly, gave me Ativan and three "trigger point" injections in my back, listened sympathetically while I told her my story, in condensed form, right up to the cerebral hemorrhage. Astonished, we compared notes. And just like that, I had a new friend and ally, someone who'd been right in the heart of the mess in the Middle East, who knew exactly what I was talking about.

I recovered from that little setback in the parking lot, too. And just in time for me to be a witness to major events on the world stage that make me prickle with a sense of what I can only call pre-PTSD.

As this was being being written, two major unfolding news stories had my riveted attention. They might not seem immediately connected, but they were.

A new Supreme Court justice, Brett Kavanaugh, had just been seated after a huge national brawl, locking in a five to four "conservative" (and I use the word advisedly) majority on the court for what looks like many years to come. The uproar during Kavanaugh's confirmation hearing, about teenage drunkenness and attempted rape and all the rest of it, should never have happened at all, because he should have been excluded from consideration long before. The whole sorry demonstration wasn't for naught, though. With his reaction—the shouting, weeping, self-pity, and lashing out—he provided us with a live performance under the klieg lights that he can't hide or deny, an indelible revelation of character flaws that should have disqualified him from being a shoe salesman, let alone a Supreme Court justice. We're stuck with him, but at least we know exactly what sort of man he is.

Back in 2001 to 2003, Kavanaugh was an associate counsel in the George W. Bush White House when a team of lawyers worked to redefine "torture," giving great latitude to interrogators in the treatment of detainees, laying the groundwork for atrocities at Guantanamo, and later, at Abu Ghraib. During confirmation hearings before the Senate Judiciary Committee in 2006, when he was being considered for his seat on the Court of Appeals for the District of Columbia Circuit, Kavanaugh claimed to have known nothing about these so-called "torture memos" until they became public in 2004.

I find that a little hard to swallow. So did others, including Sen. Patrick Leahy of Vermont, who brought up those 2006 declarations during Kavanaugh's first 2018 confirmation hearings for the SCOTUS seat. Kavanaugh denied it all, said he never saw any of those memos, knew nothing about them, had nothing to do with drafting them, and nothing to do with shaping the policies.

If that was true, then he was one incompetent and oblivious White House counsel. What was he doing while his colleagues were busily at work making it easier for torturers to do their jobs? Sharpening pencils and making coffee? If it's not true, then he lied under oath. That alone should have disqualified him. But it didn't. So now we have a justice on the Supreme Court who likely had a hand in reshaping the rules during the run-up to the 2003 invasion of Iraq, rolling back the Geneva Convention, and loosening up the restrictions. Paving the way for Abu Ghraib. For me, his presence on the court is a personal affront, and not just because he contributed to the torture free-for-all that nearly got me killed for trying to report it, and not just because my case will probably never be heard.

No, it's because of this—he also famously wrote in a published article that a sitting president should be immune to criminal investigation and prosecution, because such a resulting criminal trial would "cripple the federal government." In other words, a president is above the law and is essentially a king.

The other major story unfolding concurrently with the Kavanaugh debacle was the torture, murder, dismemberment, and disappearance of Jamal Khashoggi, a Saudi journalist and resident of the United States who walked into the Saudi embassy in Istanbul, Turkey, in early October 2018 and never came out.

The facts, as they emerged, were stomach-turning. The man went to the embassy to get papers he needed so he could get married. While his fiancée waited in the car, Khashoggi was met by a crack team of expert Saudi assassins who'd flown in just the day before. And they brought along their own Jack the Ripper; one of them was a forensic medical examiner, a guy who knows how to cut up a human body as quickly, neatly, and efficiently as a sushi chef fillets a tuna. This implied not just that they planned to kill him, but that they planned to ritually defile his corpse, an extra ISIS-like touch that's very much "in style" these days, a medieval mentality in a high-tech world.

By the following November, the CIA issued a statement saying they had proof that Crown Prince Mohammed bin Salman (a.k.a. MBS) had ordered the hit. The president of the United States' response was a masterpiece of mealy-mouthed-ness as he simultaneously undermined his own intelligence community's conclusion, ramped up his war on the press, and scrambled to not give offense to his pal MBS. His exact words: "Maybe he did, and maybe he didn't."

Ah. But no good deed goes unpunished, Mr. President. Later in November, at the G20 summit in Buenos Aires, Trump was pointedly excluded from sitting with the big kids at the Murdering Dictators Club table when MBS and

Vladimir Putin high-fived one another with giddy grins of mutual adoration on their kissers while an ignored, dejected Trump wandered aimlessly in the background.

Justice for Jamal? Not likely. How quickly it all became yesterday's news. Half a year after Khashoggi's disappearance, his fiancée was making appearances on television, begging the world to not forget his murder, to not just let it slip-slide away. But it has. What's the connection between Kavanaugh and Khashoggi? As I see it, it's not complicated at all; the relaxed restrictions on torture, starting at Guantanamo and spreading like an infection to Iraq, with the Abu Ghraib catastrophe ripping the lid off and exposing the "liberators" as barbarians, was like a huge dose of growth hormone to Al Qaeda, which metamorphosed into ISIS. Saudi Arabia is the source, the fountainhead, of Al Qaeda/ISIS. How well I remember the Sheik telling me, after my meeting in the abandoned hospital with the Al Qaeda guys from Saudi Arabia, that their mission was not "peace and understanding," that they were "officially ferocious," meaning they had the blessing of the highest Saudi Wahhabi clerics to commit any kind of violence they saw fit.

Meanwhile, we have a president reluctant to hurt the Saudis' feelings because, as he said right out loud on national TV in the wake of Khashoggi's premeditated murder, they're such great customers at the 24-Hour Cash 'n' Carry American Weapons Mart. Way before the Khashoggi atrocity, our president, like his predecessor G. W. Bush, hobnobbed with the Saudis in an openly sycophantic way. You could tell he was impressed by their robes, their manly authority, and their unlimited cash. Never mind the twisted, bizarre irony of the fact that they were major players in 9/11, when three thousand Americans died in New York City.

MBS, the new young "progressive" Saudi leader, deals his cards selectively. He makes gestures like finally allowing women to drive cars, but he locks up dissidents and troublesome relatives, and is now known to have arranged for an annoying journalist critical of his regime to be abducted and murdered.

The fact that Khashoggi was living and working in the United States and had applied for citizenship did not, apparently, give MBS pause. We can only surmise that he was emboldened by the actions and attitude of an American president deeply invested in business with Saudi Arabia. A president who supported the horrific slaughter the Saudis waged in Yemen, selling them all the American bombs and weaponry they need to kill men, women, and children. A president who had made it known that he, too, considers journalists "enemies of the people." A president with a special bone to pick with the *Washington Post*, for whom Khashoggi worked. A president who, in the tradition of Bush and Cheney and the gang, appears happy to be complicit in the whitewashing not just of Khashoggi's torture and murder, but of Saudi Arabia's participation in 9/11. Khashoggi likely earned his death sentence because he was close to revealing something the Saudis didn't want revealed—for instance, the Saudi royal family's links to Al Qaeda and 9/11. And who knows who else might have been implicated? It's said that Khashoggi was going to be naming names, most of them Saudis, but not all of them.

Whistle-blowers, journalists, and spies are closely related species. So are dictators, theocrats, and corrupt kings—like Putin of Russia, Kim Jong Un of North Korea, Mohammed bin Salman of Saudi Arabia, and Roberto Duterte of the Philippines. What they have in common is that they are all members of an international crime syndicate who don't hesitate to rub out, mob-style, journalists and whistle-blowers and occasional bothersome relatives. And, mob-like, they love an audience and to spread terror. This makes them brothers under the skin to ISIS, who publicly and bloodily rub out anyone they deem an apostate.

Their methods reveal their mentality. Putin has used bullets to kill journalists, but he's also laced food and drink with deadly polonium, as with Alexander Livtinenko, a spy who died a slow, agonizing, fully conscious death, turning yellow and skinny before the eyes of the world. And there have been, just recently, nerve-gas deaths orchestrated by Russia in the United Kingdom. Kim Jong Un had his uncle executed by firing squad, and recently used VX to kill his half-brother in an airport in Malaysia—very public, very mob-like. And Duterte simply gives a wink and a nod to anyone who wants to gun someone down in the street, makes no attempt to hide it, reminiscent of old-time mafia hits in New Jersey that left guys dead in restaurants, faces in their plates of spaghetti.

And in Saudi Arabia, despite all the "progress," public beheadings and cruci-fixions are still very much in vogue. And then there was the bloody, brazen, ISIS-like murder of Khashoggi. They deny it, but they know we know they did it. Their denial is the audacity of mobsters.

And who admires all of these great leaders, gabs with them on the phone, and aspires to be one of them by making himself above the law, forcing on us an unqualified Supreme Court justice who has argued for exactly that sort of pres-idential immunity and who could be a crucial swing vote if a case involving the president ever comes before the court? Our own current US president, the man who would be king if he weren't constrained by our deeply damaged but still somewhat functioning Western democracy. He defended Kavanaugh against sexual assault charges with language identical to his defense of MBS: "I talked to him! He swears he didn't do it!"

Some compare Trump to a televangelist, with his big hair, his suit, his shouting, his preaching style, and millions of devoted followers who believe he was chosen by God. He's definitely got the Jimmy Swaggert thing going, and it's a component of his toxic charisma. But when I look at him, I mainly see a mob boss, a Don Corleone wannabe, eager to join the international syndicate as a "made man."

With Watergate, I saw Nixon go down. Though I have my own doubts about the honesty of the case against Nixon that was presented to the world, and that's another story, I did see forces effectively engage to remove him from office. No "rule of law" is going to remove Trump from office. He's converted the entire Republican legislature into lickspittle lackeys, led by Mitch McConnell, a more insidiously destructive force, if possible, than Trump himself.

When I heard of the death of Khashoggi—a whistle-blower standing up to the bad guys and getting abducted, tortured, and killed for his trouble—I felt a shiver of identification. I even learned that his uncle, the arms dealer Adnan Khashoggi, had attended Chico State, though way before my time. Obviously, Jamal Khashoggi suffered way, way more than I did, paid the ultimate price, but I consider him a brother and a compatriot, and I'd hate to think that I went through what I did for nothing, and especially, that he went through what *he* did for nothing.

The blood of Khashoggi is on our hands, too, as surely as the blood of poor Nick Berg, the radio tower technician beheaded in Iraq by al Qaeda, is on our hands. We invaded Iraq on a wave of lies and propaganda, and with our cruelty, greed, and sloppiness, which I personally witnessed, helped breathe life into ISIS. And now we and the rest of the world reap the bitter harvest while our president plays a coy game of kissy-face with a country that should be our sworn enemy. But business is good, and that's what counts.

We know it didn't start with Trump. He owes it all to Cheney and Bush the Elder, who got things rolling in Iraq with Gulf War 1, and later, Cheney again and his court jester Dubya and the rest of the gang, who seized on 9/11 as a gift from the gods, a massive green light to go back into Iraq with their illegal pre-planned aggression and finish the job. And it could be even worse than rank opportunism. Some of us, and I'm one of them, would not be surprised to learn of American complicity in 9/11. Trump is the natural successor, and he carries lawlessness and business über alles to a whole new level. He has no regard for the laws of his own country, so why should we expect him—or any of the autocrats he mobs up with—to have any regard for international law?

Over and over again, humanity has tried to pass international treaties meant to protect us from our own worst tendencies. In 1925, after the horror that was WWI, major nations got together and signed the Geneva Protocol, which said NO to poison gas, described at the time as the "most feared, the most obscene weapon of them all." After World War II came the Nuremberg Principles, which sought, in the wake of the criminal trials of Nazi leaders, to codify "war crimes" into international law.

Then there were the SALT 1 and SALT 2 agreements in 1972, which strove to outlaw nuclear, biological, and chemical weapons. More recently, there was the Chemical Weapons Convention, signed in 1993 in the Hague by the vast majority of the nations of the world, including the United States and Saudi Arabia, a treaty prohibiting the development, production, stockpiling, and use of chemical weapons and calling for their destruction. Over and over, we pass these laws, and over and over, we flout them. Just recently, Russians were caught in the Netherlands trying to hack the OPCW (Organization for the Prohibition of Chemical

Weapons), who were investigating the poisoning by nerve gas of ex-Russian spy Sergei Skripal. And just this past April, a nerve agent was dropped on the Syrian town of Douma, unleashing death and misery on hundreds of civilians.

*Obscene.* There's the word we've been groping for to describe the sort of grotesque lawless killing loose in the world today, ranging from the crude to the high-tech. Typhoid rages on in Yemen; you'd almost think the ban on biological weapons was being violated. VX nerve gas, far from being obliterated, is being manufactured in the world today, as are nuclear weapons. Is there any reason to think that what's left of those noble international laws meant to curb human atrocities will not be further violated?

The ghost of Stalin looms over it all. Trump gets his lessons in macho mob boss comportment from Putin. Putin, in turn, got his lessons from Stalin. Putin is a former KGB colonel; the KGB grew directly out of Stalin's People's Commissariat for State Security and also out of Cheka, an associated apparatus dedicated to the policing of dissidents. Trump, therefore, is part of the Stalin tradition, a mere couple of degrees removed. He certainly has the "theatre" of it down cold, but with his own inimitable style: an I-make-the-rules lawlessness, right in our faces, combined with loud, crude, lewd public remarks, jeers, mockery, and insults.

A small-time real-estate huckster is now on the world stage with the big boys, the seriously bad corrupt dictators and kings. But he's out of his depth, and is the more dangerous because of it. All the elements for world war are in place; a bungler like Trump could blunder into the trip-wire, the way I could have blundered into the VX booby-trap in the hut in Balad, but didn't, because I was thinking ahead.

All my life, the threat of WMD was equated with nuclear warheads. I personally think the threat from chemical weapons, VX or worse, meaning biological weapons, is as great or even greater. They are easier to manufacture, assemble, disguise, and transport than nuclear weapons.

In order to know what's in store for us in the future, we must take a hard look at the past. The technology of killing grows more deadly, efficient, and profitable all the time, and humans have demonstrated that they will toss aside laws meant to check that deadliness. The international trade in weapons becomes, perversely, the engine that drives war. If the leaders of nations have no compunction about manufacturing and using chemical, biological, or nuclear weapons, why should we expect ISIS to show any restraint?

You ask: is there any hope? Despite what I saw in Samarra, my postgraduate-degree-holding colleagues behaving like cavemen (and cavewomen; let's not leave out May), I still think the *only* possible hope is education. But we must improve the "curriculum." Without conscious, applied study, most people don't know how to read, learn, and think. We have an emergency, red-alert need for critical thinking among the general population, which must be taught, and before it can be taught, people must learn how to learn. The situation is bad the world over as far as thinking and learning go; here in the United States, we have Trump appointee Betsy DeVos as our secretary of Education, hard at work dismantling what's left of our already severely damaged public school system. The "dumbing down" of America has been going on for years, and she's delivering the coup de grâce. The rest of the world has its own various versions of dumbing-down, which include starvation, fundamentalist religion, and illiteracy.

Plots and secrecy thrive when citizens don't know how to read or think, don't know history or geography, have never been exposed to the humanities. They become gullible and malleable. How to implement a renaissance in thinking and learning is the big question, but we must do it if we are to stop history from repeating itself. I'm a patriot. I still think the United States is the last, best hope for the world, if we can just throw off ignorance and greed.

Human impulses are the same as they ever were; war and brutality are nothing new. What *is* new under the sun is that there have never been as many of us as there are now, which creates pressures and plagues on a scale not seen before. Plus we now have instant communications and weapons more deadly than ever before. Not to mention fossil-fuel (read: big business)-driven climate change.

When considering the ungodly tangle of plots, terrorist attacks, weapons deals, clandestine alliances, rollbacks of regulations, and rules of war broken and tossed aside, and we wonder why we're in the awful plight we are in, we have a useful key. There's a Latin phrase associated with identifying suspects in a crime: *cui bono?* Who benefits? It's based on the practical assumption that crimes generally benefit their perpetrators financially. A popular variation of that is the adage *follow the money.*

Whatever the riddle we're trying to penetrate, whether it's 9/11, secret arms deals, the suppression of the discovery of WMD in Iraq, the death of Khashoggi in the Saudi embassy, the placing of Trump into the Oval Office, or even my own rendition and abduction, there's a way to simplify the search for the truth: just follow the money.

*Cui bono?*

The following link will take the reader to the pertinent docket page for my case of the Supreme Court of the United States: https://www.supremecourt.gov/search.aspx?filename=/docket/docketfiles/html/public/16-1338.html.